Work hard.   Have fun.

Make History.

SELLING
SUNSHINE

75 Tips, Tools, *and* Tactics *for*
Becoming *a* Wildly Successful
ENTREPRENEUR

TONY HARTL

Greenleaf
Book Group Press

Published by Greenleaf Book Group Press
Austin, TX
www.gbgpress.com

Distributed by Greenleaf Book Group LLC

For ordering information or special discounts for bulk purchases, please contact Greenleaf Book Group LLC at PO Box 91869, Austin, TX 78709, 512.891.6100.

Design and composition by Greenleaf Book Group LLC and Bumpy Design
Cover design by Greenleaf Book Group LLC

Publisher's Cataloging-In-Publication Data
(Prepared by The Donohue Group, Inc.)

Hartl, Tony.
  Selling sunshine : 75 tips, tools, and tactics for becoming a wildly successful entrepreneur / Tony Hartl. — 1st ed.
    p. ; cm.
  Includes bibliographical references.
  ISBN: 978-1-60832-059-2
  1. Entrepreneurship. 2. Success in business. 3. New business enterprises.
4. Hartl, Tony. I. Title.
HD62.5 .H37 2011
658.11   2010931405

Part of the Tree Neutral® program, which offsets the number of trees consumed in the production and printing of this book by taking proactive steps, such as planting trees in direct proportion to the number of trees used: www.treeneutral.com

TreeNeutral®

*To the hundreds of Planet Tan employees
whose passion and ideas made this book possible.*

TABLE OF CONTENTS

FOREWORD • vii

PREFACE • ix

INTRODUCTION: What Is an Entrepreneur? • **1**

CHAPTER 1: SKIN IN THE GAME • **5**
  How a Poor Midwestern Kid Became a Big Success in an
  Unlikely Industry

CHAPTER 2: PEOPLE • **21**
  Tip 1: Decide Where to Go and Work Hard to Get There
  Tip 2: Practice "Peopling"
  Tip 3: Avoid False Flattery
  Tip 4: Celebrate Success
  Tip 5: Find a Reason to Celebrate
  Tip 6: Operate on a Foundation of Fairness
  Tip 7: Treat People Right
  Tip 8: Treat People Well, and They'll Treat You Better
  Tip 9: Choose a BDC over an MBA Any Day
  Tip 10: Power Your Business on People
  Tip 11: Pay for Performance
  Key Insights on Working with People

CHAPTER 3: PASSION • **51**
  Tip 12: Follow Your Passion
  Tip 13: Stay Hungry
  Tip 14: Never Stop Learning
  Tip 15: Bring Your Joy to Work
  Tip 16: Your Employees: Family or Team?
  Tip 17: Celebrate You
  Tip 18: Know Your ABCs
  Tip 19: Establish Action Steps
  Tip 20: Stand Out from the Crowd
  Tip 21: Lead with Your Heart
  Tip 22: Create a Captivating Company Culture
  Tip 23: Shape Your Destiny

Tip 24:   Accept No Limits
Key Insights on Bringing Passion to Your Business

CHAPTER 4: PERSISTENCE • 79
Tip 25:   Create Magic
Tip 26:   Bring a Blanket!
Tip 27:   Focus, Focus, Focus
Tip 28:   Beware of Clock-watchers, Cave-dwellers, and Can-kickers
Tip 29:   Strive for Constant Improvement
Tip 30:   Know Your Numbers
Tip 31:   Everything Matters
Tip 32:   The Three Rs for Creating a Sustainable Business
Tip 33:   Change the Game
Tip 34:   Be Willing to Make Big Sacrifices
Tip 35:   Pay Attention to the Pareto Principle
Tip 36:   A Healthy Dose of Fear Is Good Medicine
Tip 37:   Find the Right Things to Do, Then Do Them
Tip 38:   Maintain a Tenacious Desire to Succeed
Key Insights on the Importance of Persistence

CHAPTER 5: PROCESS • 111
Tip 39:   Create a "10" Member Experience
Tip 40:   Get in the Trenches
Tip 41:   Choose Right over Comfortable
Tip 42:   Develop Your Team
Tip 43:   Share What You Know
Tip 44:   Check Your Ego at the Door
Tip 45:   Build Something to Believe In
Tip 46:   Accept Responsibility
Tip 47:   Practice Compassionate Termination
Tip 48:   Keep Your Info One Click Away
Tip 49:   Utilize Business Intelligence
Tip 50:   Make Your Vendors Your Partners
Key Insights on Focusing Your Process

CHAPTER 6: PERSONALITY • 141
Tip 51:   Grace in All Situations
Tip 52:   Loyalty Matters

Tip 53: Follow Your Internal Compass
Tip 54: Learn Something New Every Day
Tip 55: Unleash Your Self-confidence
Tip 56: Always Be Personable
Key Insights on Leading with Personality

CHAPTER 7: POSITIVITY • 153

Tip 57: Always Stay Positive
Tip 58: Set Big Goals
Tip 59: Provide Real Encouragement
Tip 60: Associate with Winners
Tip 61: Follow Masterful Mentors
Tip 62: Reach Out and Reach Up
Tip 63: Befriend Your Competition
Tip 64: Find Your "Angel"
Tip 65: Create Pride in the Organization
Key Insights on Staying Positive

CHAPTER 8: PROMISE • 175

Tip 66: Concentrate Your Efforts
Tip 67: The Brand Is in the Details
Tip 68: Exceed Expectations
Tip 69: Go for "Share of Heart"
Tip 70: Design the Brand and Brand the Design
Tip 71: Expand the Brand
Tip 72: Teach a Man to Fish
Tip 73: Build a Better Brand
Tip 74: Run Your Business Like You're Going to Run It Forever
Tip 75: Know When to Exit the Stage
Key Insights on Delivering on the Promise

EPILOGUE: A Brand-New Chapter • **205**

APPENDIX 1: Planet Tan's Plan for Success • **213**

APPENDIX 2: Recommended Reading • **219**

FOREWORD

When you've known Tony for any length of time, you realize several key character traits about him. Uppermost is his passion for business and life, which is infectious. While that passion is obvious from his initial enthusiastic handshake, Tony proves his genuine zest for life by working hard, never making excuses, and maintaining an unfailing commitment to progress and positivity.

Typically, a mentor is not someone who is your own age or several years younger. But then again, there's nothing typical about Tony. For the past eight years, we have had the privilege of participating in a forum with him through the Entrepreneurs' Organization (EO) in Dallas, where we meet monthly to discuss our businesses. Tony, although not the most experienced in the forum, has become one of our most respected and valued members. He could certainly vie for "smartest guy in the room" honors regularly, and when you're with him, you feel that he is more concerned with your interests than his own. Tony exudes qualities like loyalty and integrity and does so with his own unique style.

The book you are holding contains Tony's business acumen, which is equal parts street smarts and diligent study. He has a voracious appetite for reading and studying business philosophy. This, combined with his relentless pursuit of personal and corporate excellence, compelled him to try new things in his business. His personality and passion attracted top talent to his company, but it was his vision for culture and genuine desire to see his people grow and thrive that made his business a success.

Perhaps one of the best examples of Tony's lasting influence on Planet Tan is that many of the employees who began under Tony are still there and have the same energy and enthusiasm as when he owned the corporation. If you go to Planet Tan and mention Tony, the employees light up and are quick to comment on how much they learned from him. How many of us would love to have a cultural legacy that outlives our families, our businesses, or our communities? The cultural disciplines that are a Tony Hartl standard shine through his former employees and the brand he built. When a positive culture transcends new ownership, you have created something special.

We all have stories of Tony's influence in our lives. He has helped us understand the role that focus plays in a company's success, and how every new "great idea" can't be followed if it takes away from your core business. Tips such as this have caused increases in revenue by tens of millions of dollars. Choosing Tony's best idea is like picking from among a Ferrari, a Bentley, or an Aston Martin. You win no matter what.

Another key insight from the book is Tony's recipe for creating a compelling company culture. Too many people think money is the answer when it comes to motivating top performance, but money is too easy. Tony did it through cash, gifts, trips, and once-in-a-lifetime experiences. By following Tony's example, you will become a better leader and your company will benefit. Tony's book will show you how to be in clear command of your ship and ensure that everyone believes and has confidence in where they are headed.

Selling Sunshine is about the magic of Tony's success, but it is also about the nuts and bolts of how he got there. One of the ways Planet Tan was so successful was through the use of the business metrics he designed. By breaking down data into key areas, Tony was able to understand what strategic changes to make. He propelled Planet Tan to its success with the right people who fit his culture and the right metrics to get where he wanted to go. He has shared his model effectively with many EO members. Now you, too, can use his blueprint to build your own success story.

We are all honored to be included in his book and hope that you take his tried-and-true business lessons to heart.

Sincerely,
EO Apex Forum
August 2010
Alex Chang, Cofounder and Managing Director, One Technologies
Rob Enright, President, The Ward Group, Inc.
Jason Fraser, Founder, FraserCon Concrete Experts
Alan Hunt, President and CEO, Flexi Compras
Bob Lilly, President and Cofounder, Bob Lilley Professional Promotions
Tad McIntosh, President, HumCap
Kevin Miller, President and CEO, Texaslending.com
Kevin Winters, Founder, CompanyMileage.com (current) and Payroll Associates, Inc. (1993 to 2005)

PREFACE

Mine may sound like a familiar story: My parents were divorced before my second birthday. My father took off, leaving my mother to support herself and my sister and me. She worked two jobs and struggled to provide, while my sister and I wondered when the electricity was going to be shut off again, or how long we'd have to depend on others to get to the grocery store because we didn't have a car. My sister and I grew up quickly and we grew up hungry—in more ways than one.

It wasn't easy, but my mom never once complained. From observing her tireless work ethic, I learned about motivation, initiative, and hard work. She taught me my first life lesson: You can choose to be a victim, or you can choose to make it better. Mom's positive influence has stayed with me and fueled me to this day.

With my father pretty much out of the picture, I felt a responsibility for my mother and sister. Armed with the simple formula of working hard, treating people right, and doing everything I said I would do, I set out to take care of my family and to establish myself. Failure, as the saying goes, was not an option. I wasn't sure where my path would lead, but I knew that I didn't want to struggle for the rest of my life.

The hard work, the drive, and the ambition paid off. Growing up in the Midwest impoverished and with a bleak future, I turned my life around. I started a business, I grew the business, and I eventually sold the business for millions. I retired when I was just past my forty-first birthday, but I didn't stop working.

Among other things, I now want to show the next generation of entrepreneurs how it's done—or, at least, how I did it. The book you're holding in your hands is meant to motivate and inspire young people and ambitious people of any age who are open to constantly learning and improving. My hope is that this book helps you become great at what you do and earn much more money, or that it gives you the insight to move quickly up the corporate ladder. Perhaps this book will even inspire you to do what I did: become a successful entrepreneur.

Whether you're a budding entrepreneur, corporate manager, or small business owner, I hope I can help you avoid some of the challenges I faced. It doesn't matter who you are, where you're from, who your parents were, who you know, or how you got to where you are today. Whatever your past or your current circumstances, you can write your own success story, starting now. As long as you're willing to make the sacrifices and pay the price to become successful, you can take control of your own destiny and be anything you want to be. I'm living proof.

Success is a choice. Hard work is a choice. Doing the right thing and doing right by others is a choice. The internal mantra for the company I founded sums it up nicely: "Work hard. Have fun. Make history." It's also the battle cry for successful entrepreneurship and how I got to where I am today. Are you ready to make history? I invite you to come with me as I share my experiences along the long and rocky road to success.

—Tony Hartl, 2010

INTRODUCTION

What Is an Entrepreneur?

By definition, an entrepreneur is a person who takes considerable risks. Entrepreneurs create, organize, manage, and run enterprises that have never before existed. Although there may have been similar businesses or industries, there has never been one quite like yours. That's why you got into the game—to fill a need, satisfy a demand, or provide a service in a unique way for a profit. French economist Jean-Baptiste Say coined the term in 1800, saying an entrepreneur is "one who undertakes an enterprise: especially a contractor, acting as intermediary between capital and labor."

I believe that the entrepreneurial spirit is alive and well in America, and that it's still the best way to take control of your own destiny and create your ideal life. My success as an entrepreneur and business owner is living proof that the American Dream is attainable by anyone—regardless of background or personal history.

Whether you are young or old, just starting out or well into your career, the entrepreneurial path may be your best hope for real success. It's not an easy path, but it certainly can be worthwhile and immensely gratifying. My hope is that you, too, can achieve the same satisfaction and success that the entrepreneurial road has held for me.

This book is designed to make your entrepreneurial path less rocky than mine was. There may be no easy shortcuts to success, but there are pitfalls you can avoid and wise choices you can make. Success in business and in life is rarely the result of one particular watershed event. Instead, success usually comes as the result of a series of smaller decisions made every day, over the course of time. It's those small choices we make on a daily basis that can make a significant difference over the long haul—understanding and incorporating the behaviors of success and making those smart decisions one day at a time. Obviously, success involves working hard, but it also requires working smart. Success comes with persistence and determination.

My hope is that this book inspires a new generation of entrepreneurs. While there is no set formula for guaranteed success in any endeavor, there are success-oriented behaviors that will give you an edge: tips and tactics that can save you time. There are experiences that can be shared and ideas that can inspire. There are guideposts that can point the way. There are books like this one.

Within these pages, you'll find seventy-five tips, tools, and tactics for becoming a successful entrepreneur. These ideas and strategies come from the trenches and the front lines of starting a business and building a successful company over the course of more than a decade. I know that you can learn a great deal from my experience, and it's my wish to see you profit from my successes — and learn from my failures. All of the information in this book is designed to save you time, energy, heartache, and frustration.

As an entrepreneur or small business owner, you'll experience a range of emotions and experiences as you build your business. Hopefully, the contents of this book will help you experience far more highs than lows, far more reasons to celebrate than to mourn, and far more successes than failures.

I've attempted to cover many of the challenges entrepreneurs face as they develop their dreams. In these pages, I've tried to address everything from hiring and corporate culture to marketing and branding, as well as many more of the issues small businesses and start-ups face. Within the context of building a business from the ground up, I cover sales, strategy, finances, talent acquisition and retention, advertising, promotion, and even selling your business.

We'll also discuss motivation, passion, goal setting, persistence, dedication, culture, and a range of behaviors, characteristics, and traits required to succeed as an entrepreneur. You'll find information about mentors, angels, and cultural heroes — and how to find yours. You'll learn how to find employees who are bright, driven, and committed, while avoiding Clock-watchers, Cave-dwellers, and Can-kickers. You'll learn why it makes sense to befriend your competition and why you need to run your business as though you're going to run it forever. I'll also show you how to stand out from the crowd and create a "10" customer experience in your business. We'll discuss why you'd better be prepared to "bring a blanket," and why you should consider your vendors as partners. You'll learn the benefits of having your customer's "share of heart," and why you must power your business on people. We'll discover how to exceed expectations and, finally, how to know when it's time to exit the stage—and how to plan your exit so you leave them applauding.

I hope the story of Planet Tan and the many business lessons it provides will serve as inspiration and motivation for you. Wherever you may be in your entrepreneurial journey, I'm confident that this book will help you on your own road to success.

CHAPTER 1

═══ SKIN IN THE GAME ═══

How a Poor Midwestern Kid Became a Big Success
in an Unlikely Industry

Growing up, I hated the fact that we were poor. I really detested the idea that my family never had enough money for anything but the essentials—and we barely had enough for those. Not only were our circumstances difficult; they were embarrassing. In fact, I could not even pronounce the word *poor* when I was a kid. I'd say "po," even though I heard my mom use the word a lot. I'd tell my mom not to say it. I refused to admit that that was what we were—though as I got old enough to better understand, it became painfully apparent: My family was dirt poor.

As a young kid, I guess I didn't realize just how bad the situation was. A real defining moment for me was when I was about eight years old. One day after school, I heard a knock at our front door. My mom was home, but I got up and opened the door. No one was there. Just as I was about to close the door, I noticed two bags of groceries left on the stoop. I stepped out onto the porch, but I still didn't see anybody. I brought the two bags of groceries in and showed them to my mother. She began crying. We never found out who the Good Samaritan was, but even today I'm grateful for their gesture. I still thank them.

Even though life seemed chaotic and sometimes desperate growing up, I did everything I could to create normalcy. I suppose I just wanted to be a normal kid growing up in a normal house. Though creating any kind of normalcy seemed an insurmountable challenge, I tried. I remember once when we lived in Cahokia, Illinois, the chimney of our rented house collapsed, and we couldn't afford to get it fixed. I now realize that it was probably the landlord's responsibility to fix it, but as a kid, all I knew was that our chimney was broken, that it looked funny, and that I wanted to do something about it. I climbed up on the roof and did the best I could to lay the bricks back in place, stopping only when the reconstructed chimney was leaning so much I thought it would collapse again. I then dug out a little circular garden in the yard and planted some flowers that I surrounded with the unused bricks. To me, the flowers represented something beautiful. Maybe I couldn't have the proverbial white picket fence, but I at least had one little beautiful spot in the front yard.

I'd also pick flowers on the way home from school. Usually I would collect wildflowers, but sometimes I'd just yank a few blooms from a neighbor's shrub. I'd collect enough to make a little bouquet for my mom, something that would add a little color and life to our otherwise sparse surroundings. To this day, I always have fresh-cut flowers in my home.

On Our Own

I was born and raised outside St. Louis, Missouri. My father was an aeronautical engineer for McDonnell Douglas, and my mom was a housewife. My parents divorced when I was just a year and half old, and my father moved to New York to start a new life. Mom was left to raise me and my sister, which meant she had to reenter the workforce for us to survive. My mother had been a waitress when she met my father, so she was able to quickly find a job at a local restaurant.

Mom had no college degree or formal training, but she loved her kids and had a strong sense of responsibility, so she worked constantly. She took every job she could. I can't remember my mom not having at least one job. I remember when she worked in a spice factory, and she had to get up every morning at 4:30. Even with the long hours she worked, there were times when we still couldn't pay all the bills. The electricity and water were shut off more than once. When this happened, we'd have to take a shower at a neighbor's house. We'd also have to arrange for rides anywhere that was too far to walk, because we couldn't afford a car. It was humiliating, and I was scared my life would always be a struggle for the bare necessities. I resolved at a very young age to do everything in my power to ensure that my future would be more comfortable. Though I never had a dramatic Scarlett O'Hara "I'll never be hungry again" moment, I knew for sure I didn't want to have to struggle for the rest of my life like we did in those days.

Perhaps a more important lesson was learning to reject a victim mentality, a lesson I acquired from observing my mother. As hard as she worked, she never complained; she never made excuses or blamed anyone else for our situation. Instead, she kept her promises, met her commitments, and made good on her word. If I took away anything from a tough childhood, it was my mom's example of hard work, honesty, and integrity.

The silver lining in all this was that I was really motivated. I was hungry—figuratively and literally—and, like my mother, I wasn't afraid to work. As the "man of the house," I didn't waste any time in finding after-school jobs. As soon as I was old enough—by about age eight or nine—I was working around the neighborhood, trying to make some money and help out my mom. I'd shovel snow in the winter and mow lawns all summer.

The Big, Comfy Chair

I've always been a saver. I remember at a very early age wanting to save enough money so I could buy something special for my mom. She and I had visited a neighbor's house, and they had just bought some new furniture, including a new recliner. When my mom sat in it, she smiled and her eyes lit up. It was neat seeing her relaxing in the new chair, especially since back at our house all we had was an old, worn-out couch that was pretty beat up. That's when I decided that I'd save my money so I could get mom her own nice chair.

After I had enough money saved up from my lemonade stands, lawn mowing, and shoveling snow, I rode my bike down to the furniture store where I had seen a big stuffed chair in the display window. My pockets were crammed with all kinds of small bills and loose change. I marched into the furniture store, but the salesmen ignored me. They probably figured I was just fooling around.

Eventually, one of them approached me, and I told him I wanted to buy the big chair in the window. "*You* want to buy it?" he chuckled. "Yes, how much does it cost?" I asked. So the salesman played along and walked with me to the display window. He looked at the tag and said, "This chair is $249.99." "Okay, I'll take it," I told him. Loose change fell to the floor and rolled in every direction as I pulled ones and fives out of my pockets and laid them on the table. The salesman started laughing and asked who the chair was for. I said, "I'm buying my mom a new chair." The salesman immediately stopped laughing and replied earnestly, "Well, you must be a very good son." From that moment on, the salesman took me seriously and helped me with my big purchase. He even arranged to have the furniture delivered to my house so it was there when my mom got home from work.

I'll never forget the look on my mom's face when she saw that chair in our living room. I was so proud when she sat in it; it was probably one of the best moments of my entire life. And mom was thrilled. She got herself a big glass of iced tea—the sun tea that we used to make back then—and she sat in her brand-new chair. It made me so happy to see her happy. I think that was the day my desire to look after my own family developed. The thrill that I got from giving my mom that chair was better than somebody buying me a shiny, new bicycle; it was the best feeling in the world. One of my favorite quotes that best captures the experience and my philosophy since then are these words from Og Mandino: "Remember that there is no happiness in having or in getting, but only in giving. Reach out. Share. Smile. Hug. Happiness is a perfume you cannot pour on others without getting a few drops on yourself."

Maybe that's why I've always tried to be unselfish and utilitarian. I'm fortunate that at a young age I got to experience how great it felt to use my money to benefit others. It's such a simple joy to be able to make a difference in the lives of others. I suppose I'm still that same kid who likes to save my money—the kid who discovered that it truly is better to give than to receive.

Cherish the Golden Goose

Although we certainly didn't think of ourselves as budding entrepreneurs, my friends and I were always hustling to make some extra money. My family lived across the street from a bank, and on Saturday mornings my friends and I would set up a lemonade stand and take advantage of all the built-in traffic coming through the bank's drive-through lane. We did a bang-up business!

Later I began collecting aluminum cans and turning them in for cash at the recycling center. I picked up any discarded can I saw, but I also discovered a way I could minimize the time I spent collecting and still have more cans for my effort. I talked to a few of the managers at nearby bars and asked them to save their empty cans for me. They didn't mind doing it, but sometimes they'd forget, and I'd have to dumpster-dive to retrieve the discarded empties. I'd come out of the trash bin smelling like beer, but it was always worth it when I exchanged those cans for cash.

I also continued to stash my snow-shoveling money and my lawn-mowing savings. My focus was on building my savings, not indulging in short-term pleasures. Thus, I never really bought much stuff for myself. The biggest purchase I can remember making was a lawn mower that enabled me to mow more lawns without having to borrow a mower. Actually, that was more of an investment in my fledgling business than something I wanted for myself.

I was proud of my new purchase and took care of that mower like a new car owner cares for that prized possession. Even then, I understood that if you take care of an asset, that asset will continue to work for you over time. I knew that with routine maintenance the mower would last long after it had paid for itself. At the end of every summer, a neighbor cleaned the mower for me, sharpened the blades, and gave it a tune-up. I considered this maintenance taking care of the golden goose.

At the beginning of high school, I added a paper route to my list of odd jobs. It didn't take me long to figure out that I could make more money actually selling newspaper subscriptions than by delivering the papers at five o'clock in the morning. So at fifteen, I took on my first sales job, selling subscriptions door-to-door on commission.

As I look back, I appreciate that job, because it taught me how to handle rejection. In sales, as in life, you have to get used to hearing "no" a lot—and persevere anyway. Still, I got pretty good at selling the newspaper subscriptions. Eventually, I was pulling down 800 bucks a month!

By the time I was sixteen, I had saved enough money to buy my first used car, a 1974 Grand Prix. That old baby had a sunroof that leaked when it rained and a back door that wouldn't shut properly. Passengers riding in the back seat had to hold the door shut when I went around corners; when I didn't have backseat passengers, I rigged the door shut so it wouldn't swing open at every turn. But I had transportation—and no car payment.

Having to hustle and work and save meant I couldn't be as active in sports and after-school activities as I would have liked. But that was okay, because I was practical and pragmatic; I did what needed to be done. And what needed to be done was making money and helping my family.

Aside from inheriting my mother's strong work ethic, I always managed to maintain a positive outlook; I was able to find the good in the hardships. I knew I was a survivor, and I took the initiative to change my situation, which required ambition and hard work.

I did manage to steal enough time away from working to join the high school tennis team, and I got pretty good. I bought myself a tennis racket at K-Mart, and I began to play. I loved tennis so much that any chance I got I would practice by hitting a tennis ball against the back wall of the bank building across the street from our house. With my frequent practice and instruction from my great high school tennis coach and mentor, I became the number-one seed on the team. This move up on the team only reaffirmed what I already knew: Hard work and perseverance would get me places.

Bring a Blanket

I graduated from high school at the tender age of seventeen and entered Southern Illinois University at Edwardsville, paying my tuition with money from savings, student loans, and a Pell Grant. I continued working to put myself through college, and I soon got a job selling health club memberships. By the time I turned nineteen, I had worked my way up to manager of the health club. I wasn't afraid to hustle, and I figured out early on how to successfully work a full-time job and manage a full load of classes.

One of the early lessons I learned while at the health club was about managing people. I was having some staffing issues, and rather than put up with it, I fired five people in one fell swoop. Obviously, that created a huge gap in the work schedule, forcing me to open and close the club every day for several weeks. I had to work around the clock and sleep at the club just to pick up the slack. I'd finish classes, go to work at the club, close the place down at 10 PM, and then study for a few hours. The maintenance guy would come in after closing and he'd be there until about 1 AM. I brought a blanket and I'd crash on the couch in the lobby. Then I'd wake up at 5 AM, take a shower, get the club ready to open at 6 AM, and head off to classes that started at 8:30. Believe it or not, for me this schedule was much better than dealing with problem employees.

Starting early in my career, I refused to be held hostage by employees, even if it meant taking extreme measures. I always believed that I could work myself out of any situation. I wasn't going to let the inconvenience of working longer or harder get in the way of pulling the trigger on a problem employee. You just do what's got to be done.

Later that same year, I heard that some of my fellow managers of the health club chain were earning more than I was, even though I was out-working and out-managing them. I heard that one of the other local fitness chains was looking for a marketing director, and that's really what I wanted to do. I was still in college, but my aspiration at the time was to work in an ad agency or go to law school. Looking back, I have to admit that the only reason I wanted to be an attorney was because I knew they made a lot of money. What I really wanted, deep down, was a more creative pursuit in which I could come up with ideas and pursue my own vision.

The marketing job sounded perfect. This club had been around for twenty years and was very well managed. The owner-manager had poured his heart and soul into it and made the club a big success. The fitness center was established, stable, and run like a top-flight hotel. I also knew I could learn a lot from the owner. I applied, and not only did I get the job, but the owner also gave me a company car! Best of all, he gave me a lot of freedom to try new things and come up with unique ways to generate sales. I headed up the sales effort and put other initiatives in place. Of course, being the marketing director meant I'd have to spend longer hours at the club. Even though I was still in school, I made sure I was at the club during peak hours and on weekends, so I routinely worked seven days a week.

The Crest of the Wave

About this time, I remember paying $300 to take a Charles Givens course called "Wealth Without Risk." It was a one-day seminar where they taught you how to buy homes with no money down. Naturally, being the gung-ho guy that I am, I didn't just take the class; I listened to the cassettes, studied the books, and actually put the principles into practice. I got on the phone and looked for properties, did my homework, and soon bought a $46,000 condo with no down payment.

I was just nineteen years old, but I was hitting my stride. Even though I was still in college, I had a great job, was making good money, had a company car, and owned my own place. Life was good! I also befriended a great gal at school, a cheerleader who was in my biology class. Amy had a boyfriend at the time, but we hung out together and ended up going tanning a couple of times per week.

Before that I had never been to a tanning salon in my life. Little did I know that tanning would help shape my destiny. As you might have guessed, my cheerleader friend and I ended up dating. Amy came from a supportive family, and her dad was very successful and established in the community. My relationship with her was sort of the final piece in my "stability" puzzle.

That period of my life was like the crest of the wave, the pinnacle of my early success: I had finally achieved some consistency and security. So what did I do? I immediately moved my mother in with me to get her out of her rapidly deteriorating neighborhood. You may be thinking I was crazy: I was dating a beautiful cheerleader and I asked my mom to come live with me? But then as now, there was no question what I needed to do. Family always comes first.

A Planet Is Born

I graduated from Southern Illinois University at Edwardsville in 1991, and before long I was hired as a marketing director for a small chain of health clubs based in Cedar Rapids, Iowa. We had four locations in Iowa, two in South Carolina, and one in Florida, and I was initially hired to oversee the marketing effort for the four Iowa clubs. What I didn't know then was that the guy who hired me, Dave Taylor, would not only become my mentor but also play a key role in my life and my business for years to come; that relationship would eventually transcend a mentorship to become a friendship. How could I predict that twenty years after Dave hired me, we'd be hiking together through the highlands of Scotland after I had sold my company!?

However, when I first joined Dave and the company, they were barely breaking even. A year later, Dave promoted me to vice president of sales and marketing, and I was given much more responsibility for making the clubs profitable—including the locations in South Carolina and Florida. After the promotion, I was overseeing 350 employees in three states. This also meant that I was responsible for providing organization and oversight for the branding and marketing efforts of clubs in three very different marketplaces.

I made a few moves pretty quickly, such as reducing payroll by taking over management of the out-of-state locations in South Carolina and Florida. We also changed our business model from a prepaid membership model to pay-as-you-go. That was a better strategy for the health clubs and led to as many as 300 percent more signups. Once we were able to sell more pay-as-you-go memberships, we could focus on customer service and retention tactics. Our service orientation replaced the former high-pressure sales tactics the clubs had been using. I also used some of my marketing budget to reinvest in the facilities, which improved the customer experience. In a short time, we went from breakeven to netting a seven-figure profit.

Eventually, I was ready for an even bigger challenge and the opportunity to manage a larger business, so I moved to Denver at the age of twenty-six to become vice president of sales and marketing for a chain of tanning salons that operated thirty-six tanning facilities in four different markets: Denver, Cleveland, Columbus, and Dallas. It was a young company that was growing fast. As it turned out, the company was growing too fast, which led to a shortage of cash.

Not long after I joined the company, the founder announced that the company was having severe financial problems. The person who recruited me for the job called me with a "good news/bad news" scenario: The bad news was that the budget was not in line with what was being produced, and this financial instability meant they didn't have a need for my position anymore. The so-called good news was that they would keep me on if I could help sell the stores.

I had no experience as a business broker, but I needed a paycheck, so I said, "You bet!" In the process of trying to sell the businesses, I connected with one of the investors who owned a small accounting practice. I thought he was pretty sharp, so I approached him about buying some of the locations with me. I said, "Look, what do you think about buying this company?" He asked, "Do you think you could make it work?" I told him that I had a great idea for how we could make the company really succeed. Of course, he wanted to see my business plan—but I had never created a business plan. Undaunted, I took out some school notebook paper, and I scrawled out my concept on one sheet of paper.

I faxed it to him, and he called me back and asked incredulously, "Is *this* your plan?" I was undeterred and started explaining my vision to him. I said: "This concept can work, but we have to do it differently. We've got to set it up so that people have unlimited tanning at a set price. We need to provide great service and a superb experience. We need to have marketing." I told him it would only cost $40,000, and

I'd put in $10,000. Fortunately, I had ten grand in my 401(k) from my previous job, and that's what I used to start the company.

With $50,000, we bought three tanning locations in Dallas, and that was the beginning of Planet Tan. The truth is we could have made an offer for any of the four markets where the company I was working for owned facilities. In fact, the Cleveland tanning salons were doing the best; the Cleveland market may have represented the best business decision, but for me, it was also a lifestyle decision. Dallas was by far my ideal choice. It was a large, cosmopolitan city, but it still had Midwestern charm. It was also a fast-growing city with a lot of energy and excitement, everything from major sports teams to beautiful women. (Hey, I was twenty-six years old and single!)

When we first purchased the Dallas locations, all we could afford to do was change the name on the signs. I came up with the name Planet Tan, and we had a logo designed for $50. With our new name, three locations, and eight employees, we launched Planet Tan on May 11, 1995.

Creating Immediate Buy-in from the Team

The first thing we did was make sure everyone on the team wanted to be there and was willing to do whatever it took to create success. Unfortunately, it did not take very much time to realize that some of the people weren't willing to give the extra effort required to be successful. In a short amount of time, I was interviewing new people to join the team.

Next, we needed to create a hospital-clean environment for our tanning centers. In a business that requires members to take off their clothes and lie on the equipment, cleanliness is a major concern. Many on our team were young and, understandably, didn't want to be on their hands and knees cleaning behind a tanning bed, washing windows, vacuuming, or sweeping, let alone cleaning the toilets. But these are the things that our members cared about, so our priority was to create a place both we and our members could be proud of.

At first it was challenging to convince some of the team members, especially the young guys who wanted to focus on selling, of the importance of their contribution to the cleanliness of the salons. I quickly realized that if I carefully explained why their contribution was important, they were more compelled to pull their share of the load. Often, leadership begins with explaining, creating a compelling reason for people to do something, and having them do it because they want to be part of something bigger than themselves.

Once these initial expectations were in place for our team, it was much easier to focus on sales and marketing, because the people coming in to check out our business were going to receive five-star service in a clean, friendly atmosphere—and they were willing to pay for it. Plus, with the great service, they were more likely to recommend us to their friends.

Planet Tan took off so well that we opened one of the first fifty-bed tanning salons in the industry. The fact was that we had so much business, we needed to expand our locations. This was key to our strategy: We first invested in our current locations, always ensuring that our facilities and service exceeded our members' expectations. The cost of expanding our three locations could easily have gone into opening three new stores, but this would not have been in line with our strategy.

We realized that by expanding a proven location, we could serve as many members as most tanning salons see at two locations. However, unlike the other salons, we could do it without doubling the staff. Furthermore, by investing in our existing locations, we found that we could create an over-the-top experience for our members: ultimately a killer proposition that was very difficult for competitors to challenge. The end result of our early growth strategy was that we had more options, a laser focus on our business plan, sparkling facilities that members felt comfortable in, and the most up-to-date equipment in the industry—all under one roof!

Those early decisions allowed us to grow our per-unit sales to the highest in the tanning industry—and that's where they are to this day. True, we would eventually open additional locations, but only after the existing ones were doing great financially and running with superior teams in place.

Another benefit of focusing on our original locations was that out of those tightly functioning teams came our new store managers. We slowly started adding a facility every year—and in the last years, a few more than one per year—but there were times in the fourteen years I ran Planet Tan that we did not acquire a new location, because I was not satisfied with our level of success at providing value to our members. I simply would not add any additional stores until I was 100 percent sure that it was time to grow.

I'll admit it: At times my stubborn insistence on growing only at the right time may have been frustrating to other people on the team who saw markets that did not have a Planet Tan. Still, I would not add any new locations until our current members were consistently enjoying a world-class experience provided by a world class-staff; if we needed more time to correct issues, then we were going to wait. We eventually built the company up to seventeen locations; Planet Tan #17 was about to be constructed when I decided to sell the company.

I'm not really sure there was a single big reason that Planet Tan was the most successful tanning chain in the history of the industry. Understand that we produced the highest per-capita sales per unit that had ever been generated, setting records that still stand. Though it was never specifically measured, I would also bet that we would rank highest in the industry both in employee and member satisfaction.

Each Planet Tan location averaged close to $1 million in sales annually. To put that in context, compare the industry average of $200,000 per unit; the top 10 percent of stores average around $500k per store. Admittedly, our stores were bigger; we were in a major market; we had long hours of operation; our marketing budget was almost double the industry average; and we paid our people significantly more, plus providing insurance and a 401(k). But we believed in doing whatever it took to be the place people thought of when they thought of tanning.

People would fly into Dallas just to get a look at a fifty-bed tanning salon that was doing over $1 million in sales. I mean, we had people coming in, posing as customers, and looking at what "these guys were doing in Dallas." My staff would get upset at first, because often the visitors would eventually let on they owned a tanning business out of state—and many times in the Dallas community! I guess my staff thought they were taking unfair advantage, trying to scope out our strategy for success.

But I never minded. In fact, they could have simply called and I would have had someone show them our business without their having to take time pretending to want to become a Planet Tan member. I knew that the answer was not the size of our stores; if that was all it took, they could just open a 5,000-square-foot retail location and put fifty tanning beds in, then watch the business come running.

But the truth is that quantity of beds was only part of what made our company special. The success came down to diligently recruiting the very best staff we could find and empowering them with ways to stay engaged, satisfy the members, and feel that they were part of something that mattered. We always wanted our team members to know that their opinions made a difference. By staying focused and not trying to go into other lines of business, we were able to refine our entire business process in order to meet our ultimate goal: producing the world's greatest sales. We did this by training a world-class team to provide world-class service.

Planet Tan produced amazing sales numbers year after year; we set goals of double-digit same-store sales increases year over year, because we knew there were other opportunities we had not fully capitalized upon.

If there was a single key to our success, it would have to be focusing on only the few things that really mattered. Each day, my job was to avoid letting distractions take us off course. More than anything, we focused on staying true to our principles and values.

If you think about it, there are hundreds, if not thousands of small choices or decisions that each of us in business faces during the course of a year. My philosophy was to look at each decision and determine whether it took me toward my goal or in some other direction. This type of deep focus over a long period of time will allow a business to better serve its staff and customers. True, each business must change and adapt, but not in a reactive way; not because something has caused you to change your focus. Change is necessary—if it means getting better. Change is good—if it puts your business in a position to win. There are times when if you don't adapt and change you will be left behind.

Planet Tan certainly changed during my fourteen years of ownership, but the changes never took us away from our single-store mindset, from asking the central question: Are we growing sales and profit at each location? Without this strategy and focus it would have been impossible to reach the revenue levels we did. In fact, I had a "Big, Hairy, Audacious Goal" (BHAG—more about this in chapter 7) that each store at maturity would achieve 35 percent or more in EBITDA (earnings before interest, taxes, depreciation and amortization)! Many businesses are satisfied if they can achieve 15–20 percent in EBITDA, but we set our goals higher. As a result, we had locations doing over $1 million in revenue and many doing in excess of 50 percent EBITDA.

Setting and achieving such goals requires intense focus. Sure, having a clear plan is the first step, but more important than anything is your ability to stay focused on implementation. The fact is, the best plan doesn't always win—the best implementation does! I never got caught up in any sort of ego trip about who came up with what idea; I just wanted to see who could implement a winning idea that produced results.

Every business needs to figure out ways to compete and win. Usually, these success behaviors involve sales, operations, marketing, finance, and strategy:

- In sales, your main objective is to convert the customers coming in to check out the business into full-time members who can become evangelists for the business.

- With marketing, you want to create potential customers who may want to become members; you also want to reenergize current members with your message, which positively reinforces them to continue as members.

- Your finance philosophy should ensure that you are investing in ideas and people that create the biggest upside for the business.

- A successful strategy asks: What are the three to five things we are going to do this year to win?

- With operations, you need to make sure that the business is ready each day; that you have processes in place that will ensure that each customer's visit is as good as the last, making sure the business runs smoothly.

But no matter how good your strategy is, no matter how flawless your financing plan or your marketing practices, it always comes down to the people you hire to execute your plans and carry out your strategies. I believe, as much as I believe anything, that all success is caused by your people. It shouldn't be surprising, then, that the first topic we'll discuss in depth is people.

CHAPTER 2

PEOPLE

It's often said that a person is only as good as the company he keeps. This is as true in personal settings as it is in professional ones. To be the best business, you have to recruit, support, and retain the best employees. People are the driving force of any company. After reading this chapter, you will know how to find the best talent, effectively use incentives, set the tone for the company, and infuse fairness and integrity in all that you do.

It's true in almost any business (and in a service-oriented industry such as Planet Tan was a part of, it's true in spades): If you don't have energized staff who feel great about where they work and what they are doing, you will ultimately fail. This is why, in my mind, the people always come first. It's impossible to have amazing success without a successful, fired-up team.

As I mentioned in the last chapter, our unbelievable sales results had almost nothing to do with our pricing or the size of our facilities. Those things certainly helped meet our objectives in support of our goals, but trust me: If we had fifty-bed tanning salons being run by uncommitted, lackadaisical employees, Planet Tan would have looked like an empty tanning bed warehouse.

Because of our focus on people, we always wanted Planet Tan to be the employer of choice; out of all the different businesses someone might choose to work for, we wanted them to say, "I've heard Planet Tan is an awesome place to work." We wanted prospective team members to be excited about applying to work for us.

How do you get that kind of motivation and desire in a young workforce? Here's how: by getting people with the right attitudes on the team, by providing them with the tools to do a great job, by involving them in the mission, by listening, by providing them with opportunities to grow personally and in the company, and by never failing to let them know when they are doing a great job.

Tip 1

DECIDE WHERE TO GO
AND WORK HARD TO GET THERE

*Plans are only good intentions unless they immediately
degenerate into hard work.*
— *Peter Drucker*

"Work hard. Have fun. Make history." If you were part of the Planet Tan Team, those were words to live by. Those six simple words were the internal battle cry for the company I founded. But make no mistake: This was not some cutesy mission statement that we dreamed up in a conference room and then filed away to never again see the light of day. We practiced it; we breathed it; we lived it. If an applicant made it through Planet Tan's grueling screening and hiring process, he or she personified the internal mission every single day. Our mission was people focused; that was what gave it its power.

When creating your mission statement, you are deciding where you want to take your company and how you're going to achieve success. I always found it to be important to have short and succinct statements that capture an entire idea. This helps team members remember the company's mission — and helps to guarantee that each of them internalizes it.

Your mission statement also needs to generate enthusiasm when being discussed, and it needs to be lived and exhibited by everyone. Starting with the leaders of the organization and going all the way down to the most junior employee, everyone has to see and feel the mission statement. You'll overhear snippets of discussions that will indicate how the mission statement is being "lived" in your organization.

Let's break the Planet Tan mission statement down into its components and see how it contributed to the culture of success that we created.

Work Hard

This may seem obvious, but Planet Tan was not looking for Clock-watchers, Can-kickers, or Cave-dwellers. (I'll explain what a Cave-dweller is a bit later.) As a member of the elite Planet Tan Team, employees were expected to work hard, work smart, and work like they meant it. We searched for remarkable individuals who were never afraid to get their hands dirty, to get down into the trenches, to do whatever needed to be done, and to find a way to make good things happen. Honest, simple, hard work was the backbone of our company.

Have Fun

Of course, along with our first commandment of working hard, we also believed in playing hard. When we worked, we worked our tails off, but when we played, we played all out, and we had fun. It's one thing to tell your people to have fun at work, but it's another thing entirely to create an environment that cultivates a fun workplace. I would explain to my team that since they were physically at work eight hours a day anyway, they should bring their positive spirit along with them and make the most of the day; as long as they had to be at work, they might as well enjoy the workday. Bring your whole self, I told them; bring your joy, your smile, and your laugh. I did everything I could to convince them that if you make someone else's day, you'll find that you might just make your own!

Having fun was a vital part of our corporate DNA, because a happy employee makes the member experience better, which, in turn, makes for a happier member. When you're able to have fun and enjoy your work, you will feel better and your clients will feel better. Why? Because they can sense the energy and the vibe of pleasure and enthusiasm that you give off; that atmosphere of fun is electric and contagious. Everyone wins when people are having fun at work and enjoying their days. I'll go into more detail about this when I explain the Planet Tan vision for cultivating a great work environment.

Make History

Can people at a tanning company really make history? If it's Planet Tan, they can—and did! From day one at Planet Tan, we set out to make history. That may sound strange for what was formerly a mom-and-pop industry with a marginal reputation, but our bold and brash company attitude helped us shatter perceptions about the tanning business and, in the process, we often made history.

Planet Tan accomplished many "firsts" in the industry. For example, Planet Tan was the first tanning supercenter, or megastore. We completely changed the game by taking a big-box retail mentality and applying it to our small chain of tanning locations. We were also the first—and possibly only—tanning company to ever grace the cover of *Fortune Small Business* magazine. We were the first tanning company to have our ad campaign featured nationally in *Ad Age* magazine. We were undoubtedly the first small local tanning chain to hire big-name, national talent to work for and with us (more on this later). And we were certainly the first to create strategic partnerships and associations with NFL, NHL, and NBA-affiliated organizations such as the Dallas Cowboys Cheerleaders, the Dallas Mavericks Dancers, and the Dallas Stars Planet Tan Ice Girls. (Did you catch that? The Planet Tan Ice Girls!)

We took an innovative and cutting-edge approach to our business and our industry, and that resulted in our garnering a litany of "first-evers," from breakthrough advertising to groundbreaking business practices. One example that I've already mentioned was our provision of thirty to fifty tanning beds per location—absolutely unheard of in the tanning industry before we burst onto the scene.

In fact, before Planet Tan joined the industry, the average revenue of a tanning salon was just $175,000 annually. In 1995, Planet Tan smashed that ceiling when one of our stores did more than a half-million dollars in revenue. Eventually, we were the first company in the industry to break $1 million in revenue per location.

The fact is, making history is really not that daunting when you change the rules, innovate constantly, and set a new standard. When you set out to make history every day, the results will speak for themselves.

Tip 2

PRACTICE "PEOPLING"

Hide not your talents/They for use were made/
What's a sundial in the shade?
— *Benjamin Franklin*

Our focus on our people paid off just as we hoped, as evidenced by the fact that Planet Tan was consistently voted one of the best places to work in the Dallas–Fort Worth area by the *Dallas Business Journal*. We weren't able to achieve this overnight, and it certainly didn't happen by accident. From day one, we always believed that talent was our most valuable asset, and we went to great lengths to find and hire only the very best employees.

A lot of companies talk a good game when it comes to talent acquisition, but in my company, we were absolute fanatics about "peopling." As I've already suggested, if you boiled it down to the basics, the equipment and choice of tanning products were essentially the same at the majority of ours and our competitors' locations. Any salon could have expanded to match our 5,000-square-foot "big box" with its fifty tanning beds. As I've said, the only thing that really separated us from the tanning salon down the street was talent.

We knew that if we had talent—and if all our competition had was employees—we would be the more successful business. We made sure that our talent could do the work of three of our competition's employees. This approach gave us the ability to better compete so that we could attract still more talented employees. We looked for real go-getters with great attitudes, and then we would give them the necessary skills. In fact, job applicants for Planet Tan who had worked for another tanning salon already had a strike against them, because we knew that they hadn't been trained properly—or, at least, hadn't been trained according to our high standards. We felt that un-training them might be more difficult than trying to teach newcomers the Planet Tan way from the ground up.

From the beginning, one of the key metrics we used was a "revenue per full-time employee" model. I'd tell my managers, "If we need nine people, let's hire five and pay them like seven." This strategy would enable us to pay our employees more because we needed to hire fewer people to accomplish the same results—or better. The team members would win because they would make more, and the company would win because we still saved on overall payroll costs. The members would also win, because they got the benefit of having the very best, most motivated team members serve them and offering advice. It was a winning triangle. However, the only way this strategy could work was if we had truly great team members. We continued to use this metric the entire time I was at Planet Tan, and we refined our standards and benchmarks over time as we discovered what had the greatest impact.

When the time came to add new team members, we looked for outgoing people who were filled with passion and a desire to get things done; we looked for winners and action takers. During our interviews, we'd watch for the candidates who leaned forward in their seats, eager to hear more and become a part of the company. We had a long and detailed hiring process that weeded out the weaker applicants. (There will be much more on that unique process later.) There's even a "disclaimer" on the Planet Tan website that cautions applicants:

CAUTION!

Slackers and sliders just DON'T fit the mold here!
So *p-l-e-a-s-e* bring your bag full of energy, enthusiasm, and an undeniably tough work ethic with you if you want to apply! A good sense of humor is a must. You have to be a natural smiler; if you're not, it just won't happen, trust us! We are too busy having fun to engage in office politics and internal "gotcha games," and for the right people that's **HUGE!** So if this sounds like a Planet you want to be part of, spread your wings and shoot us your resume. And don't be afraid to brag! We offer remarkable opportunities for ridiculously passionate people.

As I've said, there was never any question in my mind that our people came first, because the staff was the necessary ingredient for providing extraordinary, unforgettable service to our guests and members. We knew that the experience of the members would be enhanced by the way our staff felt and performed, but we also knew that you can't train someone to be happy and outgoing; you've got to hire happy and outgoing people, then train them for the job.

From the beginning we taught our employees a way of serving our guests and showed them what that experience should look like. We also made sure that every team member had a growth plan that would provide him or her with a potential career path. Team members received regular performance feedback, and because we hired the right way, they were the type of people who were always open to improving themselves and their job performances; in other words, the feedback fell on eager ears! Our peopling program kept team members engaged and excited about their opportunities with the company.

The peopling program came down to four elements: attraction, acclimation, development, and care. Let's take a closer look at these four elements of the Planet Tan peopling program and think about how you can incorporate these into your hiring process.

1. ATTRACTION

Our employee attraction philosophy was that we never stopped recruiting talent. We wanted to always have a "virtual bench" of talent, so we always had a pipeline of prospective new hires. Of course, we also had created an ideal profile for each position within the company, so we knew exactly what to look for. I'm sure you've heard the "sales ABC" maxim: "Always be closing." Planet Tan's version of the phrase was "Always be interviewing."

As a growing company, we were constantly on the hunt for ideal talent, and who better to work for you than someone who's already drinking the Kool-Aid: someone who knows the product, uses the product, and believes in the product? In other words, oftentimes our best employees started out as our best customers. Why not? They were already fans and had an insider perspective on the company.

In fact, one of our very best team members started out as one of our top customers. Lori, from our Frisco, Texas, store, was a "raving fan" before joining the Planet Tan Team. She came to work for us and covered the morning shift, typically our slowest time. Still, by the following year's end, Lori had become our top seller, sweeping all of our internal awards for sales and customer service. Do I really have to tell you why she was so successful?

Sixty percent of our new hires came from referrals and current members. We offered big bonuses for employee referrals, since that was a rich source of prospects. In addition, we were constantly advertising on the radio, on our website, and in stores to recruit new talent. The process never stopped, because we always wanted to have that bench strength we were looking for.

2. ACCLIMATION

We referred to our process of getting our new employees up to speed quickly as our "on boarding" process. We developed ways to bring new hires on board and integrate them as quickly as possible by providing the tools, resources, and support to set them up for success. If you've shown up for a new job on day one and your employer didn't have your office ready or your business cards printed, then you know how awkward and unwelcoming such unpreparedness can be. At Planet Tan, we made sure that new team members felt welcome and acclimated immediately: We had their business cards waiting, along with a welcome card signed by their fellow employees. They were introduced to the culture and briefed on our team approach and company expectations. With proper acclimatization, our new team members could hit the ground running.

3. DEVELOPMENT

Of course, once they were on board, new team members had to be developed. We approached team-member development with the idea that confidence would lead to competence, so we took learning and development of new hires seriously. We used a buddy system in which each new employee had an advocate, that is, a person they could go to who held a similar position at another location. This meant that each new team member had a manager and an advocate whom they could call on for help and support as they learned the ropes. With this strong support system in place, each new team member was set up for success from day one.

4. CARE

Caring for employees was an important aspect of our peopling program. Once we found the best talent, we retained them through differentiation. In other words, we provided different incentives and rewards based on performance, level of responsibility, and tenure. Our "care" philosophy was based on the fact that the best people should get the best opportunities.

We were a performance-based culture that rewarded results and recognized value, and we made sure that our best talent knew that they had plenty of what we called "runway opportunities," or opportunities for growth within the company, in front of them. Leaders were groomed to grow into bigger roles within the company, and our top performers were given lots of room for growth and success.

The team members who became leaders were those who understood that they had to invest in themselves and continue to grow. As a business, we understood that the future of the company depended on filling the pipeline with future leaders and preparing them for the position they would occupy in the future.

Now, when you have a growing company, it's a lot easier to keep your people jazzed about new opportunities for growth because everyone is thinking about the new job opening, the new location getting built, or the new positions being created.

But what happens when your company is in a maintaining and improving phase instead of a rapid growth phase? You still need to keep your top performers motivated and your up-and-comers excited about the future. How can you maintain a "fast-growth energy" culture in an environment where you need to maintain and mature? Remember, rapid growth isn't always the answer.

We were able to retain the best and brightest team members—in both growth and maintaining/improving phases—because we made sure they knew that there was a clear growth path and plenty of potential for moving up within the organization. In addition to career opportunities, we made our top performers "rock stars" within the company by pouring on recognition, celebrations, and bonuses. Also, above-average compensation motivated our staff and led to retention and longevity. Note that we didn't just pay them more—that would be like throwing money at a problem and hoping it got fixed. Instead, our champion team members had more overall pay because the top performers were paid very well for *results that aligned with the goals of the company*. Team members worked hard, but they also were able to have fun and celebrate success—as you'll learn in an upcoming section!

Tip 3

AVOID FALSE FLATTERY

Teach me neither to proffer nor receive cheap praise.
— *King George V*

Nothing undermines a leader's credibility more than false flattery. Handing out cheap praise as casually as giving kids candy on Halloween will get you nowhere as a manager, and eventually your team will lose respect for you. No one likes to be patronized, and most people can usually see right through false flattery.

General Álvaro Obregón Salido of Mexico, who started out as a farmer and ended up becoming president of Mexico in 1920 after a brilliant military career, had these words inscribed on his statue at the Chapultepec Castle in Mexico City: "Don't be afraid of the enemies who attack you. Be afraid of the enemies who flatter you." The general got it right; flattery gets you nowhere. Cheap praise is shallow, disrespectful, and insincere.

On a few rare occasions, we had a manager who used flattery to gain popularity or garner support. This is akin to tricking people into liking you, and it's ultimately damaging and unsustainable. Those who use false flattery and disingenuous smooth talk for their own selfish purposes are usually found out over time, and once they have lost the trust of their people, they are doomed. These inauthentic people don't last in business once they've gained a reputation as phonies. Don't fall into this trap! Be authentic and honest with your praise.

On a related topic: As a leader you are sometimes forced to make difficult decisions. Do you want to be popular, or do you want to do the right thing? There are times when you can't have it both ways. Say what needs to be said; do what needs to be done. Don't pull any punches, and your people will respect you. You may not always tell them what they want to hear, but it's better than losing their trust and respect.

Sir Richard Steele, an eighteenth-century British author and politician, may have put it most eloquently when he said, "Whenever you commend, add your reasons for doing so; it is this which distinguishes the approbation of a man of sense from the flattery of sycophants and admiration of fools."

Tip 4

CELEBRATE SUCCESS

The more you praise and celebrate your life,
the more there is in life to celebrate.
— *Oprah Winfrey*

The "Have fun" part of our mission statement was anything but lip service. As I mentioned briefly before, we took our fun seriously. We looked for reasons to celebrate, and we commemorated even small victories. Business has to be fun; otherwise, for those folks who show up for work every day, it's just a job. After all, people are spending a significant part of their lives on the job, so celebrations can be a great way to energize the business and help make work more fun.

Once we hired new team members, we welcomed them with open arms as part of the Planet Tan Team. They were greeted at the store with balloons and a huge cardboard sign that the entire staff had signed. The manager of their location would take them to lunch or for coffee to welcome them. We'd give each new team member two picture frames and ask them to bring in pictures of people and places that inspired them. We'd even joke that there was no commitment from the company until we saw their pictures. In a way, we were kidding, but it really was important to us that team members felt a sense of belonging at Planet Tan.

We used a lot of positive reinforcement and always celebrated every success. In the early days of the company, we'd go each month to a restaurant to celebrate the top salespeople. We'd have a nice award made, call the top salespeople up to the front of the room, recognize them in front of their peers, and then hand them a cash bonus. Everyone had a blast, and, of course, every member of the team would work even harder for a shot at the "top grosser" award the following month. As the company grew, many of the recognition and rewards events took place at the store level, for the important reason that we wanted to find ways to speed up and personalize the recognition. We also continued to hold monthly meetings and annual events that became increasingly more fun over time as we learned more about what everyone enjoyed.

We did learn one lesson about what not to do. One year we decided to hold our annual kickoff meeting at midnight at Studio Movie Grill, a theater that also serves as a restaurant. During our kickoff meetings we recapped the year, shared new growth plans, and then threw a big celebration during which we handed out awards.

This particular year, we asked the Planet Tan staff to wear pajamas. We hired laser lights to flash in the sky; we asked the theater to put the words "Featuring Planet Tan" on the marquee; we had the Dallas Mavericks Drummer Band kick off the evening; and we provided a full buffet.

Everything started out great until the hypnotist showed up. One of his tricks was to hypnotize the entire audience. With the party starting at midnight and all of our staff wearing pajamas, the hypnotist was easily able to put them to sleep! So, in order to communicate our upbeat, exciting challenges and goals for the coming year—we first had to wake up the audience! We really had to work hard to communicate everything we wanted to present that evening.

Finally, though, our staff came to life when the awards part started.

The meeting ended at 2 AM! We decided never again to host a pajama meeting at midnight with a hypnotist—but we never stopped celebrating successes.

One way we continued to acknowledge high achievers was to hang plaques with the names of our award winners on the Planet Tan Wall of Fame at the corporate office for all to see. The wall was just one more way to publicly acknowledge our team leaders.

Tip 5

FIND A REASON TO CELEBRATE

Motivation is the art of getting people to do what you
want them to do because they want to do it.
— President Dwight D. Eisenhower

Not only did we zealously celebrate our success at Planet Tan; we also went to great lengths to create a positive, supportive work environment. Encouragement, recognition, and rewards were provided as often as possible. Our goal was to ensure that our staff was motivated and inspired to achieve excellent results. We worked hard at finding reasons to celebrate.

I maintained a personal goal of sending out at least five thank-you or encouragement letters every week. The letters were mailed to the employee's home so that the person receiving the note could share it with his or her family. Or, I might send it to the location as a way to recognize the entire team. I'd even send letters to team members' parents or spouses. In fact, I was at a longtime staff member's home recently, and I noticed one of the letters from years ago. The note, proudly displayed on the wall, was further proof to me of the importance of demonstrating appreciation of an employee's efforts.

January 5, 2001

Dear Mr. and Mrs. Petersen:

I have had the good fortune to work with your son Tom for just over one year. Tom took the Manager in Training position, even though he had many years in managing hotels. There was no open position at the time, but we liked the energy and attitude that Tom had.

We have recently offered Tom our first managing partner position, and believe he is most qualified for the position.

Tom is the foundation of our Management Team! In our work together, we have spent many hours at the store and on the phone. We have developed a camaraderie that transcends a pure business relationship and blends into a mentoring based friendship. I sincerely enjoy Tom; he has a work ethic second to none and an understanding of the service business and business acumen far beyond his years. I have spent my lifetime, it seems, in business working with executives at all levels and I can say to you that Tom is a man that I know you are both proud of. I share your pride in this bright and capable person, and I look forward to working with him over the next several years as Partner. I promise you that I will mentor him and share whatever I can with him to best develop his natural talents. Tom has a bright and promising future as Partner with Planet Tan Inc. I wanted you to know that I share your pride in his accomplishments, and that he is well on his way to achieving the goals that he has set for himself.

My best wishes for a Happy New Year.

Sincerely,

Tony Hartl
Chief Executive Officer
Planet Tan Inc.

To celebrate a store reaching a milestone, we began a company tradition of sending the team a cake along with our congratulations. Every year, I'd also send out a Mardi Gras King Cake to each store as another fun company ritual. Celebrations became part of the culture at Planet Tan.

After we had been in business for a few years, I launched an annual contest that ran for three months during our peak season. Everyone on the staff had a chance to win an all-expenses paid trip to Cancun, Mexico. The team members loved the idea and got really excited about the possibility of winning an all-inclusive vacation with some of their coworkers. Most of the employees were young and Mexico was close by, so they were thrilled with the opportunity. The contest was based on results and structured so that team members wouldn't be competing directly against each other; we wanted as many people as possible to make the trip.

We based the contest on sales, service, clean stores, and teamwork. Each store could accumulate points based on these criteria, along with "secret shopper" scores. We'd send a secret shopper to each location to report on the experience at the store. This kept our team members on their toes and also helped us discover any areas that needed improvement. If individuals surpassed their target numbers by thirty percent or more, they were also allowed to bring a guest to Cancun with them.

In order to totally level the playing field and give all team members a fair shot at winning our contests, we went to great lengths to adjust the scoring based on store size and volume. That way, the smaller locations wouldn't be penalized simply because they weren't set up to accommodate the same volume of clients as the larger stores. Because we set it up so that everyone had an even shot, we got buy-in and excitement from team members across the board, regardless of their position within the company or of the location of their store. We actually wanted lots of winners, so employees were never pitted against each other, and there were a variety of ways to accumulate points in the contest.

In the early years, we had all the scores faxed in so we could track the leaders. Eventually, we computerized the entire process, so that the sales scores were updated and posted on our company intranet every fifteen minutes. Having the scores in real time and up on the store computers built excitement and created a high level of awareness of the contests. Everyone on the team could see the numbers, so they could kick it up a notch if they wanted to improve their scores.

The corporate office staff could also compete in the Cancun contest if they hit certain numbers and service benchmarks. There were a few years when the entire corporate staff went, myself excluded, since I wanted them to have a good time without their boss watching over them. That was a long three-day weekend! With all my staff gone, I quickly realized how many things I didn't know. Talk about having an appreciation for customer service! I've never been so happy to see anyone as when my people came back after that long weekend!

The Cancun trips were a big hit and a great incentive to motivate the staff. Of course, nothing makes a team member happier than cash, and we certainly spread it around to the team members who helped move the company forward.

Company meetings were also often an occasion to celebrate and recognize our team members. One of the most memorable meetings I ever held was on May 11, on the company's twelfth anniversary. I called every general manager and district manager and all maintenance and corporate office support staff to thank them for their contributions. We had achieved consecutive growth for every quarter since we had been open. During the meeting, I thanked each of them for being on this journey with me and for sharing my dream to start and grow a successful company.

Since my goal was always to surprise and delight my team members, I also came up with a plan to recognize employees who had been with the company for nine or more years. During the anniversary meeting, I placed a metal briefcase on the podium, and then I called up one of my longtime employees and handed him a stack of ten $100 bills. He burst into tears, causing the rest of the managers to wonder what had happened. I then called up the other longtime staffers and also gave each of them $1,000 cash. We handed out $17,000 in cash bonuses that day. It was an amazing way to let my team know that I appreciated them and the job they were doing to make Planet Tan successful. These special meetings showed everyone how much they had achieved as a team; they became memorable, "wow" events.

In your business, there are more than likely many reasons you can begin celebrating today. Think of someone who has gone above and beyond her normal responsibilities and write her a note—not an e-mail, but a handwritten note. Also, come up with an idea for a celebration ritual that reinforces the values of your company and tell your staff it will be taking place at the end of the week. Remember: What gets reinforced gets achieved.

Tip 6

OPERATE ON A FOUNDATION OF FAIRNESS

*Live so that when your children think of fairness
and integrity, they think of you.*
—H. Jackson Brown Jr.

Maybe it's the Midwestern values instilled in me growing up, but I've always tried to conduct myself and my business on a foundation of fairness. In order to be successful in an honorable way in business, you must operate from a platform of fairness and integrity. I realize that there are plenty of other business books that espouse a take-no-prisoners attitude, but for me, being fair and ethical is paramount.

What I'm talking about is fairness across the board, whether you are dealing with an employee, a client, or a vendor. It means being fair to people who may be in what you or others consider a weaker position. It involves being fair when you don't have to be and even when nobody's watching. It means doing the right thing because it's right, not because it's convenient.

If you don't operate from a solid platform of fairness and respect, then, regardless of your business, you will ultimately fail. This may not happen in the short term, but eventually questionable ethics will doom you.

When you find yourself in a position of power over someone you're dealing with, you should take precautions not to bully or take advantage of them. It makes more sense to be fair and equitable to everyone. After all, if you took advantage of every situation and person who crosses your path, then people are either going to end up resenting you or trying to figure out how to get back at you. Plus, the situation may be reversed at some point, and you will want people to treat you with the same fairness with which you treated them.

I enjoyed the negotiation process while at Planet Tan, and as I mentioned, I always operated from a platform of fairness. My approach to negotiation was to take as much time up front to discover what the other person really wanted and then find concessions that both parties would feel good about. It never made sense to me to beat someone down in a negotiation, because it would result in the other party walking away feeling defeated or taken advantage of — and definitely not looking forward to our relationship. We wanted partners, and we wanted to make them partners for the long haul.

Of course, when negotiating with vendors, our team was always instructed to get three bids and to make sure that they were comparing apples to apples when negotiating. But I also advised them to actively look for ways to provide something that would benefit the other party other than a price concession. You'd be surprised at how many meaningful concessions you can make in a negotiation that don't involve your checkbook. I always felt that creativity and careful listening could help us find ways to sweeten the pot for our vendors and other trading partners. For example, sometimes we were able to advise our vendors and other entities we did business with, sharing best practices and ideas for becoming more efficient and profitable. The only expense to us was taking the time and trouble to find out how we could help them, but the loyalty and consideration we got in return was worth every minute we invested in the effort.

Also, we didn't always necessarily go with the lowest price, because at the end of the day, we were more concerned about the long-term relationship. "Win-win" may be a cliché, but if you invest time and careful thought in a negotiation, everyone really can walk away a winner. I always tried to emphasize to my employees that they should treat both vendors and colleagues with respect. Bullying and taking advantage of someone speaks poorly of you and your company, and that was definitely not the kind of reputation we were building. If you treat people as partners, you've got a partner and a friend instead of a potential enemy—and that can really pay off during difficult economic times or when you're in a tough spot for some other reason.

Tip 7

TREAT PEOPLE RIGHT

No act of kindness, no matter how small,
is ever wasted.
—*Aesop*

The other side of the fairness coin is simply to treat people right. You would think this would go without saying, but too much of business today is about winning at the expense of someone else or stepping on others just to get ahead. I'm not just talking about the extreme examples like Bernard Madoff or Kenneth Lay at Enron, either; I'm talking about everyday respect, loyalty, and consideration.

In Tip 6, I talked about the importance of treating people like partners, of establishing and nurturing relationships with everyone with whom you work, including vendors. Some in the business world might advise trying to get the best deal no matter what or exploiting your vendors to "get one over" on them. My advice is just the opposite: Treat people right. Make them partners. Nurture a long-term relationship. For example, I had vendors I stayed with for over a decade—in good times and bad. Even when I could have left them for much better deals, I stayed loyal and committed to that business relationship—and it paid off.

When Planet Tan was just starting out, I had one vendor for tanning lotion. They were a local company, and they gave me good terms since the business was just ramping up. Of course, as we grew, there were plenty of other lotion vendors who wanted our business, but I never forgot that early gesture, and I stuck with that one vendor for years. Even my accounting people thought I was nuts, because I could have made a much better deal with someone else. But to me, loyalty and the relationship were more important.

One important by-product of that loyalty was that my team saw how I dealt with people, and those values trickled down to my staff. The way you treat people sends a big signal to your colleagues and coworkers, because how you do anything is how you do everything. Respect and loyalty work both ways, and because my team knew I was loyal, they were loyal to me and to each other. Treating people right—across the board and top to bottom—builds an atmosphere of trust, and you can't put a price on trust!

The other obvious benefit of the "treat people right" philosophy is that it fosters cooperation and teamwork. It also makes good business sense. Think about it: If you bend over backwards to treat your team members right, they are going to be in a better frame of mind to treat your clients right. Again, everyone wins. Take good care of your people, and that translates directly into better client service. Happy employees foster happy clients.

A staff who are engaged, enjoying themselves, and learning is a staff who create a positive work environment. At Planet Tan, treating people right created a culture where employees could thrive and take better care of our guests. It would have been impossible to offer the level of service that I wanted to offer our members if that vital first component, an energized, empowered, confident staff, had not been taken care of.

We always treated people right, and we took especially good care of our team. As I've already detailed, there were celebrations, opportunities for growth and advancement, and a truly supportive culture.

Team members understood that they were respected and valued. They knew that we'd do everything we could to help make them the best person they could become.

By the same token, never act with a quick temper. It's true in all relationships in life: Once something is said, it's difficult to take it back. Before you say something you might regret, think it over or take the night to sleep on it. If you feel the same way in the morning, have a conversation about it.

On the topic of communication, I also believe that for the good of the team, a leader must be transparent; he or she must speak frankly and avoid playing games. Games take time and cost money. People who work in environments where games are going on become worried about how they should act, as opposed to discussing what the real issues are. Openness must be a two-way street. If you set an open, trusting tone as the leader, trust will be gained and communication will start flowing freely, which will speed up the positive results and satisfaction for everyone.

Finally, don't have a "shoot the messenger" mentality. If you want everyone to feel comfortable telling you what's going on, you've got to have an open-door policy and be approachable. If your team members don't think they can trust you with bad news, you're going to have some severe—and possibly fatal—gaps in your managerial information. No business can afford to always act on partial knowledge, so make sure you're approachable . . . no matter what.

Above all, remember that treating people right is not just good manners—it's good business.

Tip 8

TREAT PEOPLE WELL, AND THEY'LL TREAT YOU BETTER

One who knows how to show and how to accept
kindness will be a friend better than any possession.
— Sophocles

If you see a theme developing over the last few tips, you're right: Kindness, fairness, respect, and integrity are some of my core values, and, I believe, a big reason for my success and the success of my company.

When you are considering how you interact with people, keep in mind that treating people right does not mean letting them walk all over you. Being a kind, cooperative team player does not give others the right to take advantage of your good nature. I convey this message with a framed quote from Sonny Barger, the founder of the Hell's Angels, that I have hanging in my office behind my desk. It reads: "Treat me good, I'll treat you better. Treat me bad, I'll treat you worse." I believe that in a lighthearted way, this quote sets the relationship tone for people I'm meeting with for the first time.

That quote also says a lot about how I conduct business—tough, but fair. "If you treat me good, I'll treat you better than ever" has become one of my guiding philosophies. I will give you the benefit of the doubt, but once you've treated me bad, the party's over! If nothing else, it gives certain people a chance to reconsider ever treating me bad! Without question, I'll always prefer the carrot to the stick . . . but I've got the stick, just in case.

Treat me good, I'll treat you better; treat me bad, I'll treat you worse. Simple as that.

Tip 9

CHOOSE A BDC OVER AN MBA ANY DAY

The quality of a person's life is in direct proportion
to their commitment to excellence, regardless of
their chosen field of endeavor.
— Vince Lombardi

Bright, driven, and committed: that was the kind of person we looked to hire at Planet Tan. Since our people were unquestionably the key to our success or failure, we didn't just interview and hire staff, we had a long and comprehensive hiring process to identify only the most ideal candidates. When it came to finding the right people, we were practically fanatics about it.

We asked the following questions to determine whether the applicant had the BDC traits we desired:

1. **Bright:** Is she intelligent? Can she think on her feet? Is she able to make smart decisions?

2. **Driven:** Does the potential team member have internal drive, and is he in it for the long haul? Is he a self-starter and self-motivated?

3. **Committed:** Would she be the type of employee who was obsessed with our mission? Would she stick to a project all the way through? Did she have a track record or history of long tenure at her previous job?

We definitely hired for attitude and trained for the job. The individuals working for Planet Tan had to be bright, driven, and committed as well as enthusiastic, outgoing, cheerful, ambitious, and hungry for responsibility. In addition, to make the Planet Tan Team, they'd have to survive our grueling interview process.

As the company got bigger and we needed additional staff for new locations, we developed a hiring matrix and a detailed system for filtering job applicants. The process started the moment a job applicant walked in the door.

Whenever I was looking for a job when I was young, I knew that I had to go in prepared and expecting an interview. Even if I was there just to pick up an application, I was ready in case they offered to interview me on the spot.

At Planet Tan, we looked for people who were prepared for an interview as soon as they showed up to fill out an application, people who exuded professionalism. Did the candidate come in dressed like he might get an interview? Did he look like he wanted the job? Was he neat and well groomed?

The next filter was the application; it had to be filled out completely—and neatly. A sloppy application would put a candidate out of the running right off the bat. Aside from our insistence that an application be filled out completely and neatly, we checked that applicants answered questions properly and that their availability lined up with our needs. Candidates who did not meet these criteria were weeded out immediately. By this point in our review of applications, about half of the applicants would be disqualified.

We followed a comprehensive interview matrix we created for our managers to ensure consistency and continuity throughout the organization during the interview process. If an application passed inspection through the application process, then he or she would be invited in for an initial interview with the location's manager. This phase was really more of a screening process than a formal interview, but it gave us a chance to get a better sense of the candidate's potential.

During that initial interview, the manager would ask five standard questions to determine if the applicant was a fit for the position. Then we had the applicant take an online assessment. Our top employees from the company had already taken the same test, so we could formulate simulated test scores and use them to benchmark for a prediction of performance. That way, we were comparing prospective employees with our best and brightest who had already proven themselves. If an applicant rated well on the assessment and the manager approved, the candidate would be invited back for a more formal second interview with the store manager and the district manager.

Keep in mind that the online assessment took at least forty-five minutes for candidates to complete, so that in itself was another filter. By this point in the process our candidates had made a professional initial impression, had completed an extensive application, had filled out a detailed online assessment, and had interviewed twice. We assumed they really wanted the job if they were still gung-ho at this point. In fact, it was standard for us to begin with fifty applicants, filter that number down to twenty-five, then twelve, then six; and finally, one or two finalists. It was a grueling process, but being ultra-selective always paid off.

Some attributes, such as drive and commitment, are not trainable—you've either got it or you don't. That's why a BDC beats an advanced degree any day, as far as I'm concerned.

Tip 10

POWER YOUR BUSINESS ON PEOPLE

Great ability develops and reveals itself increasingly
with every new assignment.
— *Baltasar Gracian*

Planet Tan's intensive interview process and hiring matrix helped us build an outstanding team. Aside from the interviews and assessments, we always looked for the "lean-forward" people. We wanted the candidates who were on the edges of their seats—the ones who were bright-eyed and outgoing, ready to take on the world and make things happen. We had to find the people with the right attitude and personality because, as I've already said, you can't really train for personality.

We looked at the job interview as a first date. Obviously, the candidates would be on their best behavior and try to make a good first impression. But what would happen after the initial meeting? Was it all downhill from there, or would they be able to sustain that great attitude? For us, the emphasis was very much on talent by design, not on hiring by chance. We believed—and got repeated confirmation—that if we put in the time on the front end and got a good hire, then our likelihood of success was that much greater.

We built our business on people, realizing that having a great team with low attrition would save us money as well as set us apart in the minds of our members and the public. Unfortunately, many stores in the tanning industry are staffed by disinterested, very young hourly employees who probably put in minimal effort to get a paycheck. We had a mixture of young and not-so-young—up to seventy-three years of age, in fact. (My mom worked in the office!) We were more like a tribe than a group of employees, and like a tribe, we talked the same language and shared common goals. So if something wasn't being done by one team member, the others would hold the person accountable, because they knew one weak performance would impact everyone's future. There was a deep care for each other and our mission. We not only wanted to be the best in the tanning industry; we wanted to be the best-run little company in the world—an attitude that is hard to fake for very long.

We figured out that turnover expense could be as high as $6,000–$8,000 per hourly employee. When you add to that the manager's time, the assessments, the background checks, and the training, it was serious money, even before considering lost sales and lowered morale. That's why we put such a focus on finding the right people on the first try.

The math was not difficult: We had over 100 people in the tanning consultant role in a retail industry where annual turnover far exceeds 100 percent. With a great deal of focus, we were able to take this number down to 58 percent—still high, but significantly better than our competitors. The fact is that losing employees can cost a company hundreds of thousands of dollars. Not only that, but we calculated that if we lost one of our very best people—one of our top 10 percent performers in the tanning consultant role—this single loss could cost us more than $100,000.

After a while, we replaced the term "hiring" with "talent management," since that was what we were really doing. This phrase also better captures the ongoing importance of dealing proactively with this vital aspect of business. Remember: Your success depends on your people at least as much as—and, I believe, even more than—it depends on your financing strategy or your marketing program. Why would you not spend at least as much time thinking about them as you do any other essential asset?

The other reason why our people were the key to our success was because we never considered our business to be transaction based. Instead, we understood that we were in a relationship-oriented industry. The team member who sold our customer a tanning membership was that member's point of contact; he or she became the face of the company as far as that member was concerned.

You can readily understand this by thinking about the place where you get your hair cut. You are accustomed to seeing and talking with some of the same people each time you go. We're all the same way;

we like to see people we're familiar with. At Planet Tan, we saw a direct parallel: When our stores had higher attrition or turnover, we'd see higher client attrition.

In the earlier days of Planet Tan, the company was growing quickly and we needed to staff up. Before our hiring process became more sophisticated, we'd get fifteen to twenty people at a time into a room for a group interview session. We'd explain the position and tell them frankly how challenging it was going to be; we were basically trying to weed out the less committed candidates. After the reality check, we'd give applicants a chance to get up and leave if they weren't interested. Of course, no one ever left.

As candidates showed up for the meeting, they'd sign in and get a name tag. That way, I could see who arrived first and who was late. Three questions were written on a large easel for all to see: (1) Tell us about yourself and what makes you unique; (2) What are you most proud of; and (3) Why would you make a great addition to the team? After those three questions had been asked and answered, we asked a secret bonus question: "You've just been brought on as the director of hiring by Planet Tan and you can only hire one other person. Who in this room would you hire and why?" It was a great way to discover the standouts as selected by their peers.

By the time the group session came to an end, we would have filtered the number of candidates down to two or three, whom we asked to stay behind to talk further. It was like the Marines; we were only looking for a few good men or women. Eventually, the group process wasn't practical or scalable, so we developed the more involved hiring matrix. Still, for a time, that's how we found our best people, and many of those folks stayed with us for years.

Tip 11

PAY FOR PERFORMANCE

When performance exceeds ambition, the overlap is called success.
— *Cullen Hightower*

In order to build a team that's going to embody an energetic and exciting company, you've got to keep them motivated and inspired. We did that with positive reinforcement, incentives, and rewards. We supported and encouraged our staff at every turn. We were generous in our praise and appreciation of team members who were performing at the highest levels.

It might surprise you to learn that encouragement, support, and praise were just as important as cash incentives. As philosopher and psychologist William James said, "The deepest principle in human nature is the craving to be appreciated." It doesn't cost anything to give a word of praise or a dose of inspiration. Obviously, bonuses and incentives are important, but praise goes a long way too.

We recognized and rewarded team members for strong performance. We offered opportunities for growth and plenty of ways for team members to share in the rewards and the fruits of their labor. Planet Tan had a team of real go-getters who were hungry and thrived on the chance to be rewarded based on their results. I always said that I'd rather hold back a tiger than kick a mule, and those folks who succeeded in our company were, without question, the tigers.

We always made sure that our top performers were treated like rock stars in the company: We poured on career opportunities, recognition in front of their peers and, of course, extra cash through raises and bonuses. Achieving rock star status motivated the top performers and inspired the rest of the team to work even harder in order to become rock stars in their own right.

As I mentioned previously, our compensation system was based on three important criteria: level of responsibility, tenure, and results. Obviously, rewards for tenure created loyalty and longevity at the company. Compensation based on level of responsibility encouraged staff members to continue to grow and strive for promotion, while the results-based incentives motivated employees to hit or surpass their benchmarks. Paying for performance kept our team members hungry, hopeful, and happy!

Key Insights on Working with People

- What is your company's mission statement? Does it have substance, and is it memorable and to the point? Does it accurately support your company's philosophy and goals? Is it realistic and achievable for all employees?

- There are many ways a company can celebrate success when an individual or team reaches desired milestones. Come up with a list of ways your department or company could celebrate its achievements. The list can include a range of celebration methods, from a simple acknowledgment at a staff meeting and small prizes to more lavish celebrations such as dinner, parties, and even trips.

- Have you ever taken the easiest approach to handling a situation even though you knew it was not the best approach or the right solution? Do you think you would have had a more positive end result if you had taken the more challenging course? How might you approach similar situations in the future? How can you work with your employees to ensure that they approach problems by considering the end result, not the more convenient shortcut?

- What qualities do you look for when hiring employees? How can you encourage development of these same qualities among your current staff? Do you set an example by personally adhering to the same standards you expect from your employees? If not, in what areas can you improve and make changes?

- Does your company currently meet the average salaries for your industry in your area? If not, does the company benefit from your payroll savings enough to outweigh the negative effect your low wages have on employee morale?

CHAPTER 3

PASSION

There are a lot of things a person can fake in life, but passion isn't one of them. A truly passionate person is infectious. Furthermore, ambition, optimism, and tirelessness are the natural by-products of passion. By exuding these traits yourself, you will pass this mentality and its many benefits along to your team. This chapter explains how to nurture passion and design a plan for employee happiness through unorthodox but highly effective business practices. Everything from a board meeting to Christmas bonuses can be revamped to create a company culture that rewards, encourages, and nurtures passionate people.

FOLLOW YOUR PASSION

*The happiness of a man in this life does not consist in
the absence, but in the mastery of his passions.*
—*Alfred Lord Tennyson*

Without passion, you're destined to live a life of mediocrity. Passion is the key ingredient for purpose and meaning in your life. If you settle for less, you'll get less. By following your passion, your work becomes your life's work.

Passion feeds your energy and allows you to keep going long after others have given up. It provides motivation and inspiration; it lifts you up when you are down. Passion provides focus and direction. Empowered by passion, you can play a bigger game and really make a difference.

Understand that passion is not about chasing the money—it's about pursuing your dream, and it can't be faked. It has to come from deep within—a fire in your belly that drives you to persevere and win. If you do what you love and love what you do, you cannot fail to find happiness and prosperity.

Tip 13

STAY HUNGRY

Only passions, great passions,
can elevate the soul to great things.
— Denis Diderot

It's not enough for your top performers to stay hungry; that desire to succeed must permeate every level of the organization, from top to bottom. Of course, it has to start at the top; if the leader is not energized and inspired, how could he expect the staff to be? Desire and drive are contagious, and that hunger for success has to be passed down from the CEO.

Perhaps staying hungry came easy for me, since I had a pretty tough childhood and we never had much. My mother's daily struggle to meet our basic needs fed a desire in me to do better. I was ambitious and industrious from a very early age. My motivation to take care of my family and provide a better life gave me relentless drive. In that respect, my challenging youth was a blessing in disguise.

But I managed to stay hungry even when I began finding success. I realized early on the importance of never becoming complacent, of maintaining my inner drive, and of continuing to improve and grow every single day. Fortunately, I was able to pass this culture of relentless self-improvement along to my team members. By showing up early and staying late every day, putting in as much time as the task required, and working in the trenches, I set an example for my staff that they eagerly followed. When the staff sees the boss exhibiting grit and determination, they're a lot more likely to develop that hunger themselves.

There are three types of people in an organization: people who get things done, people who watch things get done, and people who wonder what happened. The winners get things done, and they do it through personal drive and a hunger to succeed. In order to be successful, you must be self-motivated and able to persevere when things get tough. Having that "fire in the belly" will also ensure that you'll be able to stay motivated during the inevitable tough times.

Tip 14

NEVER STOP LEARNING

Learning is not attained by chance. It must be sought
for with ardor and attended to with diligence.
—*Abigail Adams*

By this point, I hope you've figured out that no matter what business you are in, people are your most important and irreplaceable asset. If that is true, then it follows that everything you do—from recruiting to hiring to marketing—ought to have the ultimate goal of building up, empowering, and promoting improvement in the people on whom you depend. One of the most important things you can do as a leader—for yourself and your people—is to cultivate and exemplify a culture of constant, intentional learning.

In fact, I'm absolutely convinced that one of the undeniable keys to success is an insatiable desire for learning. If you decide one day that you know it all or that you've got everything figured out, that's the day you're headed for trouble. Learning is a lifelong process, and the day you stop seeking new knowledge is the day you begin to wither on the vine. You must never stop learning, and you must instill this sense of curiosity and desire for self-improvement in your team. Better yet, find people who already have that innate thirst for knowledge and get them on your team.

At Planet Tan, we were determined not just to train a person to do a particular job; we were also committed to growing and developing that individual into the best possible person he or she could be. Of course, one way that growth and learning is accomplished is by setting goals, so we always made sure we had a growth plan for our team members. We wanted them to understand that there was a long track for growth ahead of them—as I mentioned, we referred to it as their "runway." We began the process with a "Traditions" class that new employees took to become knowledgeable about and committed to the company's culture, history, and principles, and it continued with a fully developed progress plan, complete with benchmarks, for every team member.

We even had a Director of Learning and Development on staff, as well as a Field Manager of Learning and Development! Some might find it surprising that a tanning company had upper management positions dedicated to training and development, but Planet Tan was definitely not your typical tanning company! We took our training seriously. In addition, we subsidized classes at Southern Methodist University's prestigious Cox School of Business. All of our learning initiatives were designed to bring out the very best in people, so that our team would be constantly improving.

Typically, passion, ambition, and a desire for constant learning go hand in hand. We knew that if we hired people with drive and tenacity, the chances were good that they'd also have a desire to continue learning and growing. Planet Tan wasn't interested in hiring mere drones or worker bees. Instead, we wanted multidimensional people with varied interests and passions. Why? For the simple reason that folks with a natural curiosity and appetite for knowledge are usually lifelong learners. We believed that bright, interesting, passionate people were the types who would find great opportunities and a path to success at Planet Tan.

In our Bronze Book, which we'll preview in the following section, we'd explain to our new team members that life is all about what you learn. We encouraged our people to learn and try something new every day, to expand their horizons, and to share what they learned. After all, life's just more fun when you're learning!

THE BRONZE BOOK

As soon as new team members were hired at Planet Tan and attended their first mandatory "Traditions" class, they received a copy of The Bronze Book. This was much more than an employee manual; it contained our philosophy and our guiding principles.

We created a smaller version of this booklet that our team members could easily carry with them and refer to anytime. Our corporate mission thus became a living, breathing playbook, to be practiced and personified by every member of the team.

The Bronze Book explained "Who We Are": "We're fun, we're hip, we're clever, we're sassy, we're Planet Tan." It also clearly defined our purpose: "To provide an affordable luxury where every body can feel better about themselves."

The booklet continued with our philosophy of leadership:

- Identify and meet the legitimate needs (as opposed to the wants) of others.
- Develop the skill of influencing people to enthusiastically contribute their hearts, minds, and other resources toward goals identified as being for the common good.
- At Planet Tan, we are all leaders.

Of course, The Bronze Book also reiterated our mission: "To grow and dominate the indoor tanning industry"; to "become world famous"; to "be the most profitable tanning company by exceeding member expectations"; to "create superior tanning facilities—nothing less";

to achieve "110 percent member satisfaction"; and to be "team members that work as a team, exhibiting a sense of competitive pride, eagerness to excel, and putting the members' needs before their own."

In addition, The Bronze Book clearly listed our core values: excellence, passion, accountability, and integrity.

Tip 15

BRING YOUR JOY TO WORK

The secret of joy in work is contained in one word— "excellence." To know how to do something well is to enjoy it.
— Pearl Buck

You can understand why it was important for our people to bring their joy to work, especially with "Have fun" as one-third of our corporate mantra. As I've already said, happy, upbeat, and enthusiastic team members generate happy clients, and these were the type of people we were looking for. Planet Tan was no place for Debbie or Danny Downers.

This is good advice for any business. I'm sure you've seen or spoken with robotic, deadbeat employees who clearly are not happy to be at their job. Whether it's the slacker kid at the fast food counter or the disengaged customer service representative at a remote help desk, these folks usually make it known that they do not want to be where they are and that they've got better things to do than serve you. It's obvious that they're not happy, and they frequently make you unhappy as well.

At best, the negative attitude of these uninspired and uninspiring individuals leaves you with a bad taste in your mouth and an unpleasant customer experience. At worst, unhappy and apathetic employees can drive away customers and eventually kill a business; they are a cancer in your organization. Fortunately, these types of individuals never survived our screening process when we hired at Planet Tan.

Our belief was that, since about 50 percent of American workers' waking hours during the week are spent at work, we wanted team members who would enjoy how they spent this time. We wanted to give them a gig that they could be proud of and feel good about. Face it: If your body is already on the job for eight hours, why not bring along your heart and mind as well? You should have the goal of doing something every day that you can be proud of: make a positive difference in a client's life; contribute to the quality of your clients' and coworkers' experience. Whatever you do, find the joy in what you're doing.

Naturally, you can't expect your staff to be happy if you're not creating an environment or a culture that promotes positive attitudes and cheerfulness. You've got to take good care of your employees if you want them to contribute to having a positive workplace. Fortunately, I spent enough time on the front lines to be able to put myself in my staff's shoes. Once I was in those shoes, I discovered, among other things, that it's not easy being on your feet for eight or more hours at the front counter—so I installed antifatigue mats. The way I figured it, it was hard to find the joy when your feet were killing you.

We made little adjustments that made a big difference for our team members—everything from putting refrigerators and microwave ovens in the break room to throwing frequent parties and celebrations. We created a culture where team members were valued, respected, and could express themselves. And, as I've mentioned, we gave them plenty of room for growth and advancement, along with opportunities for personal development.

Ultimately, it's each employee's personal responsibility to bring joy to work. However, it's a lot easier for staff members to do so when they know that they are in a place where they are encouraged and appreciated. Create a vibrant, supportive environment where employees are respected and rewarded, add encouragement to that mix, and your people will break through walls for you, accomplishing more than they ever thought possible. In the end, team members will be happy, you'll be happy, and, most importantly, your clients will be happy.

Tip 16

YOUR EMPLOYEES: FAMILY OR TEAM?

Players win games. Teams win championships.
— Bill Taylor

You may have noticed that when I talk about employees of Planet Tan, I usually refer to them as team members. There's a lot of talk in business about companies or huge retail chains that call their employees family. That may sound warm and fuzzy in a TV commercial, but I believe employees are more of a team than a family. (Unless, of course, you're running a true family business.)

I think it's important to make the distinction between a family and a team because it has implications for what kind of employees you want—and what sort of performance expectations you can set. A team is a group of individuals committed to a common goal, like a band of brothers united in a common mission. On a team, members hold each other accountable for upholding the goals and contributing to the success of the whole.

A family, on the other hand, is a group of people who are, for better or worse, linked together for life. As the saying goes, you don't get to pick your family. They may commit indiscretions and make mistakes, but they're still family, no matter what. In other words, with a family, accountability can be a trickier proposition than it is with a team, and it has to be handled very thoughtfully and carefully—especially in a true family business.

When I form a team, I want them to have competitive greatness: each person living up to their individual potential. I'm looking for hustle, a sense of urgency, staying focused, and achieving measurable results. Often, such objectives are not suitable to apply to a family, but they fit perfectly for a team.

Tip 17

CELEBRATE YOU

Waste no more time talking about great souls and how they should be. Become one yourself!
—*Marcus Aurelius Antoninus*

Part of the Planet Tan philosophy was to encourage each and every team member to become not just the best employee he or she could be but also the best person. We hired self-assured people and we continued to build their confidence once they were part of the Planet Tan Team.

We encouraged team members to be themselves and express their individuality. While many of the job functions were standardized and uniform, the people working those systems were unique and distinctive. We encourage people to "color outside the lines," that is, as long as their actions met the "Decision Triangle" test: (1) Is it good for the member? (2) Is it good for the team? (3) Is it good for the company?

When we made decisions that satisfied all three areas, we knew that our business would be fine. Reinforcing this concept with front-line staff was our key to solving issues immediately. It was important to us to be able to take care of members' and guests' requests and concerns immediately, instead of engaging in the typical corporate buck-passing: waiting for a manager to review the request, e-mailing the request to a district manager, and then waiting some more for approval by some faceless corporate officer. This type of bureaucracy kills companies and saps the morale of both staff and clients. Why play this kind of lose-lose game? Instead, do everything you can to empower your team members while still holding them accountable for ultimate results.

Now, you shouldn't confuse the empowerment of individuality for some sort of anything-goes, free-for-all approach to business. With all our emphasis on fun and individuality, for example, when it came to dress code, we were very specific about the wearing of uniforms, and we had careful guidelines about tattoos and piercings. We insisted that tattoos be covered up, and we asked that piercings be limited to the ears. We believed it was distracting, trying to talk to someone who has a metal ball sitting on his or her tongue, and we didn't want anything to be a distraction to the service we provided our members. Our philosophy was that the way someone is dressed and looks should blend in and look professional, not stand out.

Some people who interviewed to become team members had a problem with this policy, and some team members would try and push the envelope, but we never wavered. While we understood that fashions shift and styles change, our philosophy about team member appearance went to the heart of our commitment to member comfort and to providing a world-class experience every time. We wanted everyone from young hipsters to soccer moms to feel comfortable at Planet Tan and to not ever feel out of place. This small, but important decision to create an environment by design, not by chance, was a commitment I made in the early years, and we stuck to it.

But our carefully considered policy on employee appearance never diminished the core values we tried to instill in our team members: Believe in yourself and think for yourself; celebrate yourself and be the best "you" you can be; take pride in yourself and in the work you do; care about your job and about the customer; make someone's day, and you might just find that you've made your own; and power your performance with passion. These were the ideals that helped Planet Tan build a remarkable team that was the envy of the industry.

We also encouraged our members to have confidence and self-esteem. After all, Planet Tan's slogan is "Feed Your Ego!" How better to "celebrate you" than to feed your ego? Our mission was to help people feel better about themselves, so celebrating the individual was always a big part of our brand.

Tip 18

KNOW YOUR ABCs

Life is not a dress rehearsal.
— *Rose Tremain*

In this case, ABCs have nothing to do with the alphabet and everything to do with your employees. At our company, we identified team members as either A players, B players, or C players. This "report card" on all team members helped us determine where each individual stood in the company, so we could focus on his or her career path and future. Our "Top-Grading" system allowed us to create clear expectations for how team members would be rated on performance, along with what it took to move up in the company. Our system ranked employees based on values and results. Keeping the system candid and transparent prevented any perception of game-playing. There was no "buddy system" for team member evaluations; each team member knew where he or she stood in the company. This also allowed us to have a common language for everyone on the team and to identify and nurture our brightest stars while grooming the next generation of leaders within the company.

The district managers and supervisors created reports on all their team members, and then we'd review the results to determine which category each team member fell into; this ensured that they'd get the right training and development. We could also identify how they stacked up and whether they should be moved up or moved out.

What we found was that about 20 percent of the team were A players, about 10 percent were Cs, and the vast majority, about 70 percent, were B players. Usually, the B players simply needed more time, more focus, and more training and development.

A Players

Obviously, the A-list team members were the company rock stars, our cultural heroes. We wanted to make sure that they had plenty of "runway opportunities" and were receiving the recognition and attention they deserved. First, and most importantly, they had to be living the values of the company; that was a must. Our A players also hit their goals and consistently delivered. They were our future managers, and they had the brightest prospects at Planet Tan. We also made sure that they were compensated accordingly.

B Players

Oftentimes, the difference between an A- and a B-level player was consistency—the ability to always produce results. Our B players were usually very solid and had a good foundation. They had the values needed, but perhaps their performance wasn't as consistent as an A player's. Bs were valued and definitely had a place in the company, but they hadn't yet realized their full potential. Often, they just needed more time to master the position or learn the new skills needed to drive their performance to a higher level. Other times, they just needed to mature in the position they had.

C Players

C-level players were more complex and often more difficult to manage, because they fell into a few different categories. First, if it turned out that team members simply didn't live the values, they had to go. Once in a while this could be complicated by the fact that they were doing great numbers; they might be sales stars, but they didn't fit our culture and hadn't internalized our value system. This type of C player was always the hardest to let go, but we recognized that in order to achieve the kind of success we were looking for, we couldn't compromise, even for the sake of big sales numbers. If you have someone in your business who puts up great numbers but isn't living by your business's values, you must either let that person go or accept that your integrity will suffer, staff morale will decline, and your "superstar" will ultimately hurt the company. You can't be held hostage to a bad fit just because someone is bringing in business. So, even if a "culture killer" is hitting his numbers, he still needs to go.

You could also have someone who is very competent in another position, but because of her attitude she finds it hard to get along with others and creates a negative work environment. This C player could even be someone who has been with the company for a while and knows her job well, but is resistant to change. In these tough instances, we would do everything possible to get the individual to understand that a change was needed for the benefit of the company. If he or she could not make the mental shift, we would suggest that the person might be more happy somewhere else.

On the other hand, you might find a C player with a great attitude and the appropriate values, but he simply does not perform to your expectations. If his values are in place and you are convinced of his potential, the problem may be that he is in a position that doesn't allow him to work with his strengths. In that case, try to find another spot for him in the company where he may be able to succeed. If we couldn't find a place for this type of C-level player to fit, we would at least provide him with a soft landing when we let him go.

The last category of C players were the newbies or "greenies." These were the new hires who hadn't proven themselves yet; it was simply too soon to tell whether or not they would pan out as part of the team. We knew that this part of our team was constantly shifting, changing, and evolving; today's C players could become tomorrow's Bs or even As.

However you design your system for evaluating and managing your team for growth and improvement, you must recognize that this is a dynamic process. Your system must allow for individual growth and change—as well as the occasional tough decision to release someone who just isn't the right fit. Remember: You're building a team, not living with a family. Have a system in place that guarantees accountability and rewards improvement. Make it your tool for building success—not a club for inflicting punishment.

Tip 19

ESTABLISH ACTION STEPS

It's not only what we do, but also what we do not do,
for which we are accountable.
—*Moliere*

When I'm mentoring a young entrepreneur, creating action steps is always high on my list of best practices. Whether you establish action steps after a meeting for your team or at the beginning of the week for yourself, they give everyone direction and accountability. An action step is something tangible, definable, and measurable that accomplishes a small part of a larger goal.

For example, as I mentioned in chapter 2, we wanted Planet Tan to be the "employer of choice." That was our broad goal; how we got there was a series of action steps that reverberated down the chain of command. An action step at the top was creating a benefit package and level of compensation that would entice great talent. An action step at a lower level was having everyone sign a card on a new employee's first day. These actions, and many more in between, helped Planet Tan to be named the "Best Place to Work" by the *Dallas Business Journal* in 2006 and 2007. This accolade didn't come lightly or quickly. We had been in business for more than ten years, so our employee satisfaction was the culmination of a very long series of targeted action steps. We were successful because we had a measurable goal and took the time to define each step along the way.

Action steps keep you on track and keep everyone accountable. We would prioritize our steps, set deadlines, and monitor our progress. It wasn't sexy, but the most effective business practices usually aren't. There's nothing flashy about coming in early every day, staying late, and keeping a priority list in the top desk drawer. The results this discipline generates, however, can, with a bit of luck, get you on the cover of industry magazines.

One of the hardest habits to instill in entrepreneurs is a dogged focus on a single task. As passionate, positive-thinking people, entrepreneurs typically believe they can be great at everything. Action steps help to rein in the lofty dreamer and channel her passion to the most important issue at hand. Energy and enthusiasm are assets when they are put to work for a clearly defined goal. Action steps are more than items on a "To Do List"; they are focused, targeted objectives that work toward a common, defined purpose.

One example of a large-scale goal achieved through action steps is when we moved our business presence online. First, we identified high-level action steps, such as building a website and joining complementary online communities and social networks. Each of these big projects involved a series of smaller actions that included identifying the demographic for our online audience, designing a website that was consistent with the brand, and making the site easy to navigate and understand. Lower-level action steps included determining the content for our social media profiles and website, making targeted, purposeful posts, and building a strong following. It's best to start at the top and identify your overarching goal before getting down to the details. This way, you can trace each step to ensure it is in line with your goal.

Just as important as creating action steps is evaluating their effectiveness. As a rule, I establish ways to measure progress up front so that we know how we are doing as we go along. Our evaluation method is akin to having a scoreboard; it's a way the entire company can track our progress. For the online campaign, we measured our success by a few key metrics: How many "friends" or "followers" do we have? How many posts are we making each week? How many comments and "likes" are those posts generating? We could literally watch our action steps produce results as our online communities grew and became more active.

Be on the lookout for opportunities to use action steps in your company. There doesn't need to be a large initiative to justify creating action steps; it's a great tool to use for tasks big and small. By establishing action steps with your employees, you will give them a clear path to achieve a goal. Once you've introduced the idea, let them take responsibility for defining their own action steps, and then hold them accountable. The result will be a more focused, productive company.

Tip 20

STAND OUT FROM THE CROWD

Insist on yourself; never imitate.
Every great man is unique.
— *Ralph Waldo Emerson*

From day one, Planet Tan was designed to stand out from the crowd and be successful by being different. It was never our intention to be a "me too" business, and when it came to the less-than-glamorous tanning industry, that was a good thing.

At a time when most tanning salons were small, mom-and-pop operations or hair salons with one tanning bed tucked away in the back room, we burst out of the gate and onto the scene to bring legitimacy, style, and fun to the business. We were different by design, and we set out on a mission not only to stand out but also to stand far above the rest. Planet Tan was unlike anything the tanning industry had ever seen before.

Obviously, "standing out" and creating a unique, well-defined brand is vital for a business, but it can be just as important for an individual and an entrepreneur. How well you differentiate yourself from the competition could very well determine your success or failure. What makes you unique? What is your personal brand? Do you have a specific niche or a narrow target market? Decide how you're going to stand out from the crowd and be memorable while solving a problem or meeting a need that will motivate a customer to pay for what you can offer.

LEAD WITH YOUR HEART

Too often we underestimate the power of a touch,
a smile, a kind word, a listening ear, an honest
compliment, or the smallest act of caring, all of which
have the potential to turn a life around.
—Leo Buscaglia

Plenty of companies *say* that people are their most important asset, but at Planet Tan, it was so much more than lip service. We were a tightly knit team; we cared deeply about each and every team member, and we made sure that they knew they were valued.

In addition to being the right thing to do, it was also the best and only way to do business. Because we cared about our team members, Planet Tan developed a reputation as a great place to work. I've already mentioned our goal of being an employer of choice. Perhaps that helps to explain why we were named one of Dallas's "Best Places to Work" several years in a row and why we were recognized as a small business with big perks. As a result, our turnover was remarkably low, and we were the envy of the industry.

I've already discussed how we showed appreciation with celebrations, parties, contests, and rewards. More elaborate and unorthodox incentives included sending staff to dinners via limousine, our legendary employee trips to Cancun, which I've already mentioned, and . . . meetings on my boat.

There was something about having meetings on my boat that created a bond and a connection with our team. After all, it wasn't the usual, ho-hum conference room! My philosophy was that meetings were really discussions, and I liked our discussions to be relaxed and informal. So, as part of my goal to make meetings comfortable, we started "business on a boat," or "BOB" meetings. We'd have meetings or employee reviews on my boat so our discussions would be fun and casual. We also felt that a completely different environment led to more creativity and connection.

Admittedly, you may not have a boat available to use for meetings with your team. Still, try to come up with fun, unexpected, and even outdoor locations to have meetings. After all, we always thought that fresh air led to fresh ideas! Even more important, your team members will recognize that your creativity and consideration in finding different, fun places to meet is evidence of your care and thought about them and the company. And that will pay dividends you never expected.

For these and other reasons, working at Planet Tan was always more than a job for our team members. We created a caring environment where everyone had the opportunity to grow, excel, and be rewarded—both personally and professionally. One team member shared with us that Planet Tan was the only company she ever worked for where management cared just as much about her becoming a better person as it did about her doing better at her job. This was employee happiness by design, and it became a hallmark of the company.

THE VALUE OF BEING PRESENT

It's easy to get distracted in a business meeting. Whether it's looking out the window, clicking your pen, or tapping your fingers on the desk, they all communicate the same thing: I'm bored. Avoid behaviors that express disinterest; they are not only disrespectful but can cause other employees to see you as distant and unengaged. Instead, go the extra mile to exhibit active listening characteristics such as nodding while others are speaking, asking smart questions, and paying attention to the responses. Elicit feedback from all levels of employees present to check their engagement and affirm your respect and value for their opinions. It's easy to relate to those equal in standing with you, but a true leader cares about the contributions of all staff members. (Adapted from Stephanie J. Reel, "The Ten Habits of a Caring Organization: Principles Based Leadership," *EDUCAUSE Center for Applied Research*, Vol. 2006, Issue 8, April 11, 2006.)

Tip 22

CREATE A CAPTIVATING COMPANY CULTURE

*Quality is the result of a carefully constructed cultural
environment. It has to be the fabric of the organization,
not part of the fabric.*
— *Philip Crosby*

When I founded Planet Tan, I wanted to do more than start a company—I wanted to create a culture. I set out to develop an upbeat, positive, and forward-thinking work environment where great people could flourish. I intended that working at Planet Tan would be much more than just a job—it was an attitude and a belief system.

One of the ways that we fueled that belief system was by creating company rituals. We developed traditions within the company, and we used our frequent celebrations to reinforce those traditions, both great and small. Whether the occasion was a team member's tenure, hitting a sales or service goal, opening a new store, or simply passing on a great story of company success, we used company celebrations as a ritual to begin building a culture of accomplishment, positivity, and pride in Planet Tan.

For example, if we'd just reached a certain milestone or if the team had hit a big goal, I'd call a meeting for all the employees in the support center, at the end of the day on a certain Friday, and tell them I had some important things to discuss. Once everyone arrived at the meeting, I'd announce that it was "$100 Dollar Friday" and hand out $100 bills to all the staff. That's a great way to start a weekend, and a great way to keep your team motivated and excited after they've reached a milestone. We used spontaneous and unexpected incentives and rewards like this as a teaching tool to reinforce positive behavior and exceptional performance. I preferred using these types of bonuses and unanticipated rewards over things like traditional

Christmas bonuses because the spontaneous extras had far more impact and emphasized our values.

Another specific technique we used to develop our culture was to start our internal meetings by sharing a round of recent success stories. That set the tone and continued to reinforce our belief in Planet Tan as a place where success happened.

The thing is, you can't "manufacture" culture. However you decide to approach this important aspect of your business, you have to realize that culture develops over time in the things you do, the ideals you follow, and the people you hire. Creating a company culture takes time, energy, creativity, and passion.

Developing a positive company culture is much more than a warm and fuzzy concept or a buzzword in a corporate mission statement. The right culture is crucial to having a high-performing organization. You can't expect your employees to pull together and move mountains unless a strong, supportive culture is in place throughout the company. At Planet Tan, one of the ways we were able to sustain the company's growth, energy, and momentum was by having a culture that permeated the entire organization.

While you can't force or mandate culture, you can design the right environment for it to flourish. We spent a great deal of time thinking about our culture and thinking of ways to create a place where people would want to work. We asked ourselves how we could become a "destination employer" for great people. We realized that we couldn't sit back and hope that our company would end up with a positive culture—we had to proactively promote it, foster it, preach it, and live it.

How do you foster that environment from day one? Since your company is really your people, you start with making sure you've got the right team. (Remember: It's all about the people!) Are the people you hire the right fit for your organization? In our case, we looked for true team players with high energy and a strong service mentality. Are your new hires integrated into the system properly and given opportunities to quickly connect with your other employees? Do they receive the appropriate information and training to feel confident and ready to dive into their roles? Are all the right tools and resources provided to team members so they can perform well? Are feedback mechanisms in place to let them know how they're doing?

At Planet Tan, we felt it was vital to create immediate and constant two-way communication on a continuous basis. It was never enough for us to settle for the typical six-month or annual employee evaluations. We provided and elicited feedback constantly. We put systems into place that allowed us to let new employees know how they were doing. We also gave employees ways to communicate with us immediately so potential problems could be remedied long before resentment or disenchantment could take hold. In addition to that open communication, we also had regular and ongoing reviews to give our team members every opportunity to continue to grow personally and professionally.

In fact, we wanted to have in place a "cascade of communication" to keep the entire team moving in the same direction. One of our rituals was an initiative called the President's Advisory Council. PAC gave me an opportunity to meet once a month with our hourly employees. We'd also have annual kickoffs, quarterly dinner celebrations, and yearly summer picnics. And because of our association with the national sports franchises, every year we'd get a luxury suite with the Dallas Stars and the Mavericks, and we'd take our managers and top performers to the games.

We used any and every opportunity to connect and communicate with our team. By investing in technology early on, we developed our company intranet to improve our internal communication. We wanted all our stores talking and sharing constantly: communicating best practices, passing along highlights and stories . . . you name it. Any team member with something positive to share could blast it out to everyone. We gave the team ways to communicate and provided them with the tools and technology to spread the word. And this was years before Twitter and Facebook and other social networking tools made communication even easier!

I made it a point to connect with everyone. Being inclusive and being able to relate to people at all levels is an important leadership trait; you've got to show that everyone matters in your organization, and you've got to set the example.

We took our open-door policy seriously, and we made sure that each team member had direct access to me if they felt they needed it. This was not meant to circumvent the managers or supervisors, but to reinforce the cultural expectation that any member of the team could always talk to the CEO when necessary. We had notices that explained our open-door policy, both in English and in Spanish, posted in every break room at each location. The note reminded team members that they could call or e-mail me directly, and it listed my phone number and personal e-mail. We made sure the team understood that their voices could be heard and that the lines of communication were always open.

I was equally accessible to our members. Callers not only got my personal message on the answering machine whenever they called Planet Tan; I also gave them the option of reaching me directly. If members had a problem, question, or concern, they could reach me by e-mail or voice mail, and I'd get back to them as soon as I could. Members often commented on how surprised and delighted they were that the CEO personally returned their calls. This philosophy of feedback really strengthened our connection with our members and enhanced our customer service.

Obviously, we wanted our staff to feel connected and invested in the company's success. We developed traditions that would bond our employees, welding them into team members who would always have each other's backs. We did a lot of little things to keep the energy high and the atmosphere fun.

The point is, when it comes to developing a company culture that values feedback and communication, good intentions are not enough. Many companies claim to have an open-door policy, for example, but it's not enough just to say it. You've got to do what you say and over-deliver on your promises. We developed multiple ways for our team to give and receive feedback. We conducted frequent employee surveys, held our PAC meetings, and made sure that every team member had opportunities to participate.

Tip 23

SHAPE YOUR DESTINY

Destiny is no matter of chance. It is a matter of choice. It is not a thing to be waited for, it is a thing to be achieved.
— *William Jennings Bryan*

Everything you are today is a result of what you have done up to this point in your life. At Planet Tan, we made sure that our team members understood that their future at the company—and their future in general—was entirely up to them. They had the power to shape their own destinies. We gave our staff the tools, resources, support, and opportunities for personal and professional growth; whether they actually seized those opportunities was up to them.

I consider myself fortunate that I learned early on that the ball was in my court, and my future was up to me. My mother taught me the important lesson to be the best me I could be, and I took it to heart. I studied successful people, I read self-improvement books, and I constantly listened to motivational tapes. I also adopted "virtual mentors" like Dale Carnegie, Zig Ziglar, and Benjamin Franklin (I even have a big painting of Ben Franklin in my office). I thought of these virtual mentors as my imaginary board of directors or personal advisory group. As a result of studying and emulating these self-growth masters, I understood that I was in control of my own future. In fact, I never aspired to be like a celebrity or rock star—I simply wanted to be the version of myself that I imagined in my mind I would one day become. I aspired to be the better, future version of me.

FOCUS ON SUCCESS

The *Harvard Business Review* reported on a 2009 study showing that, on a neurological level, success is actually a lot more informative than failure. For instance, if you get rewarded, your brain remembers what you did right. On the other hand, when you experience failure, your brain looks for the reason why, so that you don't repeat the same mistake. So by focusing on a person's strength, you are setting them up for success and allowing them to excel. As a manager, you've got to help your people by maximizing their strengths and minimizing their weaknesses. (Scott Berinato, *Harvard Business Review*, January/February 2010.)

My virtual mentors shaped my early philosophy, but once I got deeper into my business, my reading and research shifted to thought leaders like Peter Drucker and Jack Welch. I wanted to understand more about leadership and business strategy, and classic business books like Drucker's *Managing for Results* and *Innovation and Entrepreneurship* influenced my leadership style. I read everything Jack Welch wrote, and I emulated these leaders in order to become a better leader myself.

And so, my advice is to be yourself . . . but be your *best* self. Make the decisions and take the actions that will lead to the future you deserve. You have unlimited potential as long as you're willing to take responsibility for your own life and realize that it's you—not external factors—that shape your destiny.

Tip 24

ACCEPT NO LIMITS

Nothing great in the world has ever been accomplished
without passion.
— Georg Wilhelm

When you truly care about something and when you follow your passion, there are no limits to what can be accomplished. The team we put together at Planet Tan lived and breathed the mission, and our passion to be the biggest and the best gave us unlimited potential. We took the "Make history" part of our internal mantra seriously; we played big and we refused to accept limitations.

Because of our big-thinking, larger-than-life philosophy, people assumed that we were a national company. Even though we only had a few locations, we were projecting a much larger presence. Our no-holds-barred, megastore mentality helped us attract national attention; it helped us lure big-time talent from major ad agencies in New York and put together big deals with major partners like the Dallas Cowboys Cheerleaders, the Dallas Stars, and the Dallas Mavericks. Later in the book, I'll talk about the value of associating with proven winners. Right now, I want to make the point that our ability to attract and complement such outstanding trading partners and image builders was a result of our refusal to operate according to "small business" thinking.

Once we aligned Planet Tan with the Mavs, we were very fortunate to work closely with their innovative and high-profile entrepreneur/ owner, Mark Cuban. Mark and Planet Tan were a perfect match: He embodied the fun, energetic, and optimistic attitude that Planet Tan was developing. Ryan Mackey from the Mavericks' front office was instrumental in connecting me with Mark, and he helped us create a truly unique partnership. Through a series of calls and e-mails, we developed an amazing sponsorship package. I'll also talk more about Mark and our fantastic partnership a bit later.

Of course, none of this could have been accomplished with limiting beliefs or traditional thinking. Planet Tan never considered itself simply a tanning salon; we were a tanning superstore — a destination. The typical salon had seven to ten tanning beds; Planet Tan had fifty. Traditional salons sold tanning; Planet Tan provided an experience. Most tanning salons had limited hours; Planet Tan was open from 7:00 AM to 11:00 PM, seven days a week. We were customer-centric, convenient, and fun.

We created a compelling brand and an enormously successful business because we refused to be boxed in by small thinking. We brought our passion and enthusiasm to work and used it to accomplish amazing things. We were relentless in our pursuit of constant improvement and growth. We scoffed at the naysayers and as a result, we turned an industry on its ear. All of this was made possible because we would accept no limits.

Key Insights on Bringing Passion to Your Business

- How can you continually foster "a hunger for success" with your employees? What are ways you can set an example of passion for the company? How can setting goals and making short- and long-term projections encourage a thirst for knowledge?

- There are many ways to create a passionate company culture. What are a few examples that you can implement in your office to express respect, concern, and support for your employees?

- What kind of effect can a "worker-bee" employee have on company morale? How should you deal with such employees? What are some tactics for finding joy in your work—and helping your team members to do the same?

- Why is it important to distinguish between living in a family and operating like a team? How does having a team mentality influence how you treat your employees and how they treat each other?

- Is encouraging employees to express individuality a good management principle? What are the benefits and potential downfalls of this practice? Is there a good system of eliciting feedback at your company? Do employees feel safe speaking their minds? Why would this benefit business?

- Effective evaluation is an important part of a successful business. Think about what components a good evaluation method has and how your business could specifically tailor a method for your needs. How would you identify the A-, B-, and C-level players in your company?

- What are "Action Steps"? How are they different than a "To Do List"? What area or project at your company could benefit from using action steps?

- Meetings and conferences are part of the day-to-day operations of a business, but there are ways to spice up the normal routine. What are the advantages to having an unconventional location or structure for a meeting? How does a unique atmosphere affect the participants? Brainstorm a list of places outside the office where you could host meetings.

CHAPTER 4

PERSISTENCE

It's been said that the devil is in the details. When applied to running a company, this aphorism is as true as ever. One manifestation of persistence means never tiring of analyzing data to determine how to better do business. It's not enough to merely put in long hours. They must be effective hours that contribute to the overall success of your business. The first step is identifying an evaluation model that accurately gauges company performance; the next is knowing how to use that data to hone what is already working and to strengthen problem areas. This chapter outlines the importance of persistence and its practical application in business models.

When I was starting out in my professional life, one of the things I quickly realized is that if I did a job well, I would have a job; if I knew why the job was being done, I would be a manager; and if I could inspire people to achieve mutually agreed goals, I would become a leader. The only way to get successfully to the end of this evolutionary process is through persistence. This is one of those areas where you can make a decision to create your own destiny and take charge of the direction of your career and life.

Tip 25

CREATE MAGIC

Whatever you can do, or dream you can, begin it.
Boldness has genius, power, and magic in it.
—*Johann Wolfgang von Goethe*

In today's increasingly competitive retail environment, I'm convinced that it's not enough to simply provide a product or service for customers; you have to provide an over-the-top experience—you have to transform customers into members, make them become raving fans. In other words, you have to create a little magic. Something has to happen when the public interacts with your business that sticks in their minds, that pulls them back because they want to have a repeat of the experience you created for them.

At Planet Tan, we did this by breaking the mold of what a tanning salon was supposed to look like and by training and equipping a committed, enthusiastic, confident team that was totally focused on helping members have that over-the-top experience every time they visited one of our locations. In your business, the magic may take a slightly different form—but it has to be there.

The thing to remember is that part of being an entrepreneur—maybe the central part—is creating opportunity or an idea where one doesn't currently exist. Your job is to figure out a product or service that has a market, one that you can serve better than the current players, and that offers a wide enough margin for you to make a profit. It's not easy, but it is doable; it's one part art and a huge part persistence. Figuring out that unique niche that you can fill better than anyone else, then defining your enterprise around its ability to fill it, is where the magic comes in.

Many small things will determine whether or not you create the magic—whether you will become a successful business owner and move up the ranks. What I love about being an entrepreneur is that you are your business's principal investment; the successful application of your time and energy will allow the profits to take care of themselves. That is money that goes directly to feeding the continual refinement and enhancement of your magic-making efforts, so understanding the importance of profits allows you to become even more valuable to your company by focusing on its ultimate success. Always choose to focus on ultimate success!

Tip 26

BRING A BLANKET!

Energy and persistence conquer all things.
— Benjamin Franklin

Persistence, determination, perseverance, resolve — call it what you want, but without it, failure is inevitable. Persistence is an absolute must-have ingredient to build any sustainable business. So when I say "bring a blanket," it means be prepared to pull your share of all-nighters; be ready to sleep on the sofa at the office.

This willingness has been part of my philosophy my entire working life. While I was in college and managing a health club at the same time, there were many times when I'd have to work around the clock or grab a few hours of sleep right there at the health club. Crashing on the office sofa comes with the territory if you want to run the show.

Remember that I was just nineteen when I started managing that health club, and I was carrying a full course load at college. Still, I refused to be jerked around by ineffective employees. When the time came to let people go, I decided I'd rather pick up the slack and work longer and harder than be held hostage by underperforming workers. That's why, on one occasion, I let five people go at once, even though I knew doing so would create huge gaps in the staffing schedule — gaps that I was responsible for filling.

As I related in the opening chapter of this book, I made up for the lack of staff by working extra hours myself. I'd open the club at 6:00 AM, get things rolling, and then be at my first class by 8:30. After classes, I would return to the club and work the rest of the day and night until we closed the place at 10:00 PM. After a few days of this routine, I decided it wasn't worth driving home just to show up back at the club a few hours later, so I grabbed a blanket and slept on the sofa in the lobby of the club. I knew that hard work and long hours came with being the boss, and it was worth it to me to sleep at the club rather than be saddled with bad employees.

If you want to stay ahead of the pack and find real success, you've got to be willing to sacrifice and put in the time. That means rolling up your sleeves, getting into the trenches, and when necessary, sleeping on the couch at work. If you want to be the best, then be prepared to bring a blanket!

Tip 27

FOCUS, FOCUS, FOCUS

*One reason so few of us achieve what we truly want is
that we never direct our focus; we never concentrate our
power. Most people dabble their way through life, never
deciding to master anything in particular.*
— *Tony Robbins*

Persistence requires laser focus. One vital key to success is to stay focused on the task at hand. One of my favorite quotes of all time is from Ben Franklin: "Once a job is first begun, leave it not until it's done./Whether a matter great or small, do it well or not at all."

Focus can be extremely difficult, especially for entrepreneurs and creative thinkers, who are usually "idea" people. We tend to be big thinkers with lots of imagination, vision, and new innovations. It's easy to get caught up in the next new thing or the bright and shiny objects and distractions. Fresh ideas are great, but you can't wander off in several new directions every day. To be successful, you've got to have the discipline to focus on your core business.

Time and time again, I've seen very successful CEOs and executives stray from their core businesses or try to launch unrelated enterprises, only to see all of their ventures fail. If you take your eye off the ball, then everything you've worked so hard to build will fall apart. A leader needs to set the direction and keep everyone on track. It's the leader's job to make sure people are focused on a few key items in the business and to eliminate any distractions.

We faced this challenge at Planet Tan. Sometimes we had managers who suggested that we franchise, or add a new product line, or branch out into something new. Though on the surface these might have seemed like great ideas and logical next steps, they also involved diluting our focus and ultimately decreasing our ability to meet our clients' and team's expectations. If you're rolling out a new initiative every month, it becomes frustrating and demoralizing to your people, because soon they're not sure what to focus on. I've heard friends in the retail investment world talk about the "product du jour": the latest thing that management is touting as the cure for every investor's ills. The problem with such an approach is that you can't be an expert in a hundred different things. If you try to do everything, often you end up accomplishing nothing.

I call these folks "starbursters." Loaded down with too many unrelated notions, they take off really fast and have brilliant, flashy ideas, but then the efforts fizzle. Starbursters can't focus on one thing long enough to see it through. Eventually they flame out in midair like a bottle rocket—or crash and burn.

Starbursters are bad for your business because they end up taking you in directions that de-focus and de-energize your mission. As a leader, you've got to keep your team targeted on the core business and on things that support the core business. I've also heard this referred to as "making sure the Main Thing stays the Main Thing."

It's too easy to get caught up in another line of business or with expansion into areas that distract you. At Planet Tan, we understood that we were in the indoor tanning industry, and that was our sole focus. Everything we did had to reinforce getting and maintaining members. All activities had to ultimately lead to growing the business. Our attention to the core business was not unlike Jack Welch's strategy when evaluating opportunities for General Electric. He'd ask, "Do we fix it, do we sell it, or do we close it?" That's a pretty clear sense of focus.

Another method of evaluating new ideas and opportunities is to ask yourself the famous Peter Drucker question: "If you weren't already in the business, would you enter it today?" If the answer is no, then the question becomes, "What are you going to do about it?" Again, the point is that a loss of focus can be your undoing. Know what the prize is, and keep your eyes on it!

TOP FIVE WAYS TO BE FOCUSED AT WORK

Before you can maintain your company's focus, you must understand how to concentrate your own efforts. The big picture is a business with a clear, singular mission. The smaller picture is a staff—and a boss—that understands time management and how to communicate information efficiently. Follow these five tips to increase your focus throughout the work day.

Make a To Do List: And stick to it. Having a prioritized list helps you stay on task and measure your progress.

Prioritize E-mail: Instead of dealing with hundreds of unread e-mails ranging from personal to professional, arrange your e-mail into folders and organize them by assignment, priority, and context.

Schedule Interruptions: Instead of having an open-door policy all day, block out a time for questions and concerns to be raised. You'll find you can be much more productive without people constantly walking in with requests.

Fight the Boredom: Inevitably, parts of the job are going to be repetitive and monotonous. You can best combat this by choosing the best time each day to handle these sorts of tasks. Perhaps you are most productive in the morning or right before lunch; find the ideal time for you to knock out boring paperwork or number crunching.

Choose Music Carefully: Some music can be conducive to work, but certain types can be more distracting than silence. The office isn't the place to check out the latest album or sample new music. Consider listening to an album you've heard before or instrumental music if your ears need more than the clicking of the keyboard to stay sharp.

Tip 28

BEWARE OF CLOCK-WATCHERS, CAVE-DWELLERS, AND CAN-KICKERS

*Keep away from people who try to belittle your
ambitions. Small people always do that, but the really
great make you feel that you, too, can become great.*
— *Mark Twain*

Every organization has Clock-watchers, Cave-dwellers, and Can-kickers. You know the culprits: They sit on the sidelines, ready to dash for the door the instant their shift is up. In the meantime, they either withdraw from team members and clients, expending just enough effort to avoid getting fired, or else they dish the dirt and talk about the ways things "should" be done. Here's how you can tell if you've got one of these scoundrels in your midst.

Clock-watchers

The Clock-watcher is the last person to show up and the first to leave. To him, lunch is the most important hour of the day. Only an Olympic runner could beat the Clock-watcher out the door. The Clock-watcher carefully tracks any "extra" time he puts in so he can make sure he gets back every minute. Unfortunately, he usually confuses long hours with productivity.

At our company, the emphasis was based on results, not working long hours; we didn't confuse activity with accomplishment. Sure, there were times when long hours were necessary, but we had team members who were willing to make sacrifices. They were not watching every minute on the clock to sprint out the door at the end of their shift.

The problem with Clock-watchers is that they only put in the minimum amount of work to get by, while draining the energy of their coworkers. These people slowly undermine the mission of the company, and they can also be a bad influence on the newer employees who haven't quite been fully integrated into the positive company culture. Clock-watchers can demoralize the rest of the team. You don't need them.

Cave-dwellers

Cave-dwellers hibernate in their offices or hide behind their computers. They never get out into the field or work on the front lines. They don't visit the stores or engage with customers. It's no surprise that they're not connected with the team and that they can't inspire others. They claim that they're just "too busy" to get out there and circulate, so they never venture out of their caves.

Sam Walton was the opposite of a Cave-dweller. Often referred to as the inventor of MBWA ("management by walking around"), the founder of the world's largest retail chain was famous for being out in the field, personally talking with customers, potential customers, and employees at his Wal-Mart stores. A friend of mine told a story that took place years ago in a small town in West Texas, where a new Wal-Mart was being built. A group of buddies used to gather for coffee most mornings in a fast food restaurant across the highway from the Wal-Mart construction site, and one morning an older gentleman in work clothes approached their table. He asked if he could sit down, and since he seemed pretty friendly, they told him to pull up a chair. Eventually, one of them mentioned to the new arrival that they hadn't seen him around, and asked him what he did for a living. The older man motioned at the construction site across the road. "That's my store going in over there," he said. It was Sam Walton! Instead of relaxing at his home in Bentonville, Arkansas, or even sitting in his office at corporate headquarters, he was making a field trip to West

Texas to see how things were coming along with his new store! That is true leadership—and the precise opposite of Cave-dweller behavior. So, the question is: Whom do you want working for you? A Cave-dweller, or the next Sam Walton?

As a leader, you've got to be in the field and in the trenches with your people. If you lead by example and you're willing to get your hands dirty along with your team, your people will be a lot more likely to follow you into battle. More importantly, you'll have your fingers on the pulse of the business, and you'll be able to engage and connect with your clients.

Can-kickers

The Can-kicker is always on the sidelines complaining instead of getting in the game to participate. Can-kickers are agitators and gossip-mongers. They're quick to point out what's wrong, but they are never willing to jump in and fix it. Instead, they'd rather stay over to the side, kicking their can and stirring up dust. Can-kickers can be likened to hecklers at a comedy show: They're not willing to get on stage, but they're the first to hurl an insult from the safety of the darkness beyond the spotlights. The only energy they invest is negative.

Can-kickers (as well as Clock-watchers and Cave-dwellers) didn't last long at Planet Tan, and they shouldn't have a place in your business, either!

Tip 29

STRIVE FOR CONSTANT IMPROVEMENT

Almost all quality improvement comes via simplification
of design, manufacturing . . . layout, processes,
and procedures.
— *Tom Peters*

It may come as no surprise that Planet Tan followed the Japanese philosophy of Kaizen: continuous improvement. Companies like Toyota have made the concept more popular in the United States, and personal development guru Tony Robbins has adopted the philosophy with his CANI ("constant and never-ending improvement") method.

The five main elements of Kaizen include teamwork, personal discipline, improved morale, quality circles, and suggestions for improvement. I hope that by now you can already identify these principles in some of Planet Tan's management philosophies.

Obviously, one of the cornerstones of our company was a quest for constant improvement. We wanted to get better every single day—as a business and as individuals. Our passion for performance meant that we were always looking for new and innovative ways to measure and evaluate. What can be measured can be improved, so we did our best to quantify all kinds of key indicators. We believed in reviewing key metrics by department, and then we'd work hard to improve those numbers. We used a bunch of KPIs—Key Performance Indicators—to get a read on where we could do better.

Sales were a major metric, so we kept a very close eye on our sales performance. Sales were posted daily, and eventually we acquired software that was able to track sales "live" so we could see our numbers for the day or month right up to the minute. Having immediate access to these numbers helped energize and motivate the team and gave us a great snapshot of performance.

Having the sales numbers live on screen also turned out to be a great tool to foster healthy competition among all the Planet Tan locations, since no store wanted to be in last place. It also helped motivate and improve the "middle" performers, because the numbers were on their computer screens all day and they were constantly reminded that they'd have to step it up to avoid losing ground. Of course, the top performers loved the tracking system, because they always wanted to be the top dog. They thrived on the competition and the recognition of being in the lead.

Aside from keeping score and promoting healthy competition, there were practical applications for the sales metrics, because patterns could be spotted very quickly. Since the data were live, we could immediately identify and address poor performance. By contrast, had we been getting these reports only weekly or monthly, it would have been much more difficult to respond or react to the data in a timely fashion. With live tracking, we could provide the right feedback on performance more efficiently and effectively.

Tip 30

KNOW YOUR NUMBERS

Continual improvement is an unending journey.
— *Lloyd Dobyns*

In our persistent, never-ending pursuit of improvement, we were constantly on the hunt for new and better ways to gauge our performance. Because referrals and word of mouth are the lifeblood of our business—in fact, almost any business—we started using a research tool called Net Promoter Score (NPS). NPS is a relatively simple method of measuring customer satisfaction. What it does is measure the proportion of customer "promoters" minus "detractors." The resulting score (higher is better) can be used to improve customer service and drive referrals.

NPS was developed by customer-loyalty guru Fred Reichheld, a partner in the Boston-based consulting firm Bain & Company and author of *The Ultimate Question.* The tool is used by large corporations, such as General Electric and Pitney Bowes, but we found it incredibly useful even for a business of our modest size. In fact, our use of NPS made Planet Tan the focus of a cover story in *Fortune Small Business.*

The Net Promoter Score is determined by asking customers to rate you on a scale from 0 to 10 based on the "ultimate question": "How likely is it that you would recommend this company to a friend or colleague?" Next, group the ratings: 9s and 10s (promoters), 7s and 8s (passives), and 0s through 6s (detractors). Then subtract the percentage of detractors from the percentage of promoters to determine your score. For example, a business with 80 percent promoters and 20 percent detractors would have an NPS of 60.

Follow up is key to the survey, since the resulting feedback can give you a unique view into the customer's experience and interaction with you. Some of your most useful information may even come from your detractors; they can give you constructive criticism that helps you address problem areas of your business.

From there, the idea is to continue to drive the number up and constantly improve your Net Promoter Score. While the scores can vary greatly, the average U.S. company has an NPS of approximately 15. Anything over 50 is considered a home run. The first time Planet Tan ran the survey, our NPS was 66!

Do you remember that earlier I talked about the perception of many in our market that Planet Tan was a national company, even though we had only sixteen locations in the Dallas area? Well, in this connection, I thought it was fascinating to compare our NPS score with those of some nationally known, "brand-name" companies, like the following:

USAA (insurance and financial services)	82 %
Harley-Davidson	81 %
Amazon.com	73 %
⇨ **PLANET TAN**	**66 %**
Apple Computers	66 %
Southwest Airlines	51 %
Dell Computers	50 %
Adobe (software)	48 %

This just goes to show that what we believed at Planet Tan about projecting a world-class presence and refusing to limit ourselves to small-time thinking or business approaches really did put us in a "brand-name" category with the public!

Prior to our discovery of NPS, Planet Tan used a lengthy e-mail survey to get member opinions. The survey took half an hour to complete, and our response rate was only 3 percent. When we switched to the much simpler NPS system, and our response rate rose to 11 percent, we received a great deal of clear, actionable member feedback. To automate the process, we sent out e-mails to our current members using a partnership with FishBowl, an e-mail marketing company that helped us automate the process and make immediate calculations of results. This real-time information was immensely valuable, and using it we created real-time responses and actions for improvement. NPS was also an easy concept for our staff to understand: Here's our score, and if we improve our interactions with our members, the number goes up — a good thing. It's easy to focus on one number and then work to boost it.

We always understood that our growth and success depended heavily on the member experience and member referrals, but NPS gave us an easy-to-use metric to show us whether or not we were doing well enough to rate a referral from the member. Perhaps even more important, it allowed our managers to dig deeper and find out why the detractors were unhappy. So, after our first NPS survey, we had our managers track down the detractors to get more specific feedback. The results were enlightening.

We discovered that some members found our fee structure and "credits" system confusing. Since we were selling customer credits redeemable for tanning-bed time, our guests were not always sure what the services cost in real dollars. Based on that feedback, we switched to a simple monthly membership system.

We also discovered that some of the less satisfied survey respondents felt a bit put off when they were finished with their tanning sessions. Our staff was so focused on new guest arrivals that the members who were leaving were not getting enough attention. As a result of that insight, we created a new policy I called the "post-tan affirmation." That basically meant that team members acknowledged the folks on their way out and sent them off with a compliment, such as "You got some good color today," or a friendly phrase, such as the subtly suggestive "See you tomorrow!" This one small adjustment improved the overall experience for our guests, and as a result, our NPS scores — and our sales — improved.

Information like this was vital to Planet Tan, because we also could use the research to identify key indicators and predict future results. As I mentioned, the feedback we received from unhappy members was often more valuable than the positive strokes we got from the promoters. We found that if we acted with a sense of urgency and responded quickly, we could usually resolve any issue.

If, on the other hand, the member had something good to say, we'd also review those comments and look for patterns and trends. We'd find common themes and then use the same messaging in our marketing. By using the same messaging and language that our members were giving us in their feedback, we could more effectively reinforce the positive attributes of Planet Tan in our advertising.

Tip 31

EVERYTHING MATTERS

Beware of the man who won't be bothered with details.
— *William Feather*

Part of our persistence for improvement at Planet Tan was bound up in the idea that everything—and I mean *everything*—mattered to us when it came to the member experience. As soon as possible after a member joined, we identified and defined all of the potential "touch points," that is, each of the details and places and things that made up the overall member experience.

We began this process the moment a Planet Tan member pulled into the parking lot: We made sure that our lots were clean and free of debris. The first job for the opening team member was to clean up the parking lot. Then, since the windows are the eyes and the soul of the business, we'd make sure that our windows were spotless. As members entered the store, they were greeted by friendly and gregarious front desk staff and welcomed into a bright, bold, colorful lobby. Team members would even run out from behind the front desk to open the front door for our guests. Once members were in the lobby, they'd hear music that was unique to Planet Tan. This was really a page from the Starbucks playbook: hearing music you wouldn't normally hear anywhere else. Once the member was in her tanning room, she'd have a choice of six different genres of music to listen to while she tanned. We conducted surveys twice a year to determine what kind of music our guests preferred, and we'd custom program those specific genres of music at each store location.

We also took a cue from Blockbuster and other big-box retailers and made sure that our stores were brightly lit so our members would feel safe coming and going late at night—this was especially important for our female members. All of these "small details" created an overall impression of the business. Humans have five senses, but we believed that a sixth sense occurs when you have a great experience. It's hard to define, but you know it once it has happened. All of those small touches—each possibly inconsequential in itself—add up to creating the magic that I spoke of earlier.

Tip 32

THE THREE Rs FOR CREATING A SUSTAINABLE BUSINESS

Success is more a function of consistent common sense than it is of genius.
—An Wang

Planet Tan's business model relied on the three Rs: (1) Return a member, (2) Refer a member, and (3) Recover a member. Let's take a look at the three Rs for creating a sustainable business.

Return a Member

With any membership-based business, returning the member is crucial. Not only does the member have to join; he also has to stick around if your business is to flourish. We measured how frequently members returned and what their usage patterns were like so that we could continue to engage them and give them reasons to keep coming back.

Obviously, a new member's visits to Planet Tan typically peak during the first few weeks, so we'd offer early incentives to create "enmeshment" and keep that member actively engaged. We worked on increasing the member's usage and frequency with e-mail remind-ers, loyalty programs, and other promotions. Much of our business was driven by making sure the member came back again and again and ultimately stayed with us for years.

Refer a Member

The majority of our new members were referrals from existing members. Positive buzz and word of mouth were crucial to our business—and it probably is to yours, also. Our reputation and our healthy obsession with the member experience helped spread the word and generate referrals consistently. This obsession was also inte-grated into the NPS system that we used to track and refine member satisfaction (see page 89).

Once we identified members who were using the salons consis-tently, getting great results, and enjoying an excellent experience at Planet Tan, there was a good chance that these members would become evangelists for us. We provided additional incentives and rewards for those top customers who referred others. We'd give them e-mails they could forward to their friends, guest passes, and other resources to make it easy for them to promote Planet Tan.

In addition, our member-evangelists were given the VIP treat-ment. On one occasion we recognized our top one hundred members with mountain bikes, and on other occasions we'd take the top ten members from each store to a private VIP box right on the field at a Dallas Cowboys game. We wanted to give our evangelists unique gifts and once-in-a-lifetime experiences to reward them for bringing new members to Planet Tan.

Recover a Member

We made sure we recovered potentially lost members by empowering our frontline staff to fix the issue; we refused to let a member problem wait or get worse. Planet Tan had a "dusk policy," an expectation that any member issues or conflicts would be resolved by the end of the day on which we learned of them. Our team members had the authority and accountability to address problems and take action to correct problems. More often than not, this swift, proactive recovery policy rectified member issues.

To us, losing a member was akin to losing a best friend. Our team was trained to recover the member before she canceled her membership. We kept a laser focus on recovery and used business intelligence to determine who was leaving, why they were leaving, if the issue could be resolved, and how we could reengage them.

In addition to looking at recovery on a micro level, member by member, we also looked for bigger trends or potential problem areas on a macro level. We could look at attrition by location or by manager and mine the data to identify themes. Once we'd handled such a situation, we'd transform that business intelligence into training or policies designed to reduce member attrition. These "Exception Reports" were not gotchas intended to bully or beat up our team members, but rather diagnostics that allowed us to see what someone was doing well or where improvement was needed. At that point, we could go out there and spread best practices or improvement to the other members of the team. If we saw an issue that was not good for business, we had the information needed to determine if it represented a needed training improvement or an individual, personal issue with a particular team member.

Tip 33

CHANGE THE GAME

Turbulence is life force. It is opportunity. Let's love turbulence and use it for change.
—Ramsay Clark

Keep in mind that all of these things we were doing—the extensive staff training, the focus on member experience, the research and measurement—were being done in an industry that most people at the time didn't take seriously. We were working to build something from almost nothing.

We had to literally change the game by being radically different—and radically better! We first established our internal company values: "Work hard. Have fun. Make history." Then we took them out into the world with an irreverent, hip, in-your-face attitude, beginning with our "Feed Your Ego" slogan and continuing with the member experience we created in the stores.

In a very short time, we changed the game and brought a lot of credibility to the indoor tanning industry as a whole. Suddenly, indoor tanning wasn't about "fake and bake"; it was about looking and feeling good, an affordable luxury that would help everybody feel better about themselves. Planet Tan had a very intentional brand that was designed to be trendy, fun, and sassy. By finding the right talent and building the best team in the business, we were able to personify our brand and deliver on our promise to be more stylish and cooler than any other tanning center and to provide an unsurpassed tanning experience.

As you can see, changing the game requires both an internal and an external focus. We had to develop an internal culture that would develop and support the external member experience. We had to make sure that everything we did as employees would deliver on the promise of creating 110 percent member satisfaction in the stores.

Planet Tan was able to change the game because of our competitive advantage: the incomparable member experience. Despite all the demands on our members' time, we give them a compelling reason to spend some of their time with us. In a business like ours, which relies on repeat visits, it was important that we didn't just become a transaction. That's why we focused on the relationship with the member. From culture to compensation, we cued our people to concentrate on the relationship.

As our "Work hard/Have fun/Make history" mantra implies, we really did set out to rock the tanning industry and do something that had never been done before. We never looked at other tanning salons for guidance. Instead, we studied big companies like GE and successful CEOs like Jack Welch. We'd look at Starbucks or Nike and model their success strategies. Rather than consider what the tanning salon down the road was doing, we looked at what the Fortune 500 companies were doing that we could emulate. We had a big-picture mentality, so we studied and imitated the best companies. Being a small company that thought big was definitely a game changer for us.

As a tennis player in high school, I knew that if I was a B-level player, the only way to become an A-level player was to compete against A-level players. By doing that, I became the number-one seed on my team. It was the same with Planet Tan: We wanted to be the biggest and the best, so that was whom we chose to measure ourselves against.

Tip 34

BE WILLING TO MAKE BIG SACRIFICES

Great achievement is usually born of great sacrifice,
and is never the result of selfishness.
—Napoleon Hill

Persistence is also about committing to the long haul and sticking it out in good times and bad. That requires sacrifices—sometimes big ones like time away from your personal life. *Merriam-Webster's Collegiate Dictionary* defines sacrifice as "destruction or surrender of something for the sake of something else." Speaking of the dictionary, one of my favorite tenets is, "The only place you'll find success before work is in the dictionary." Most entrepreneurs understand that making big sacrifices means giving up short-term gain for a bigger payoff in the future. You've got to be willing to take the long view, even if it means making significant sacrifices today.

Be prepared to devote long, hard hours to your craft, knowing that you will stumble and bloody yourself along the path of gaining experience. To succeed, you must love your business as if it were a living, breathing being in need of constant care and feeding. If you truly love what you do, the magic of success comes as the hours turn into days, then weeks, then years.

Success requires sacrifice, and that means if you're the boss, you're going to give up much of your personal life and focus your energies on your business. As we were building a culture at Planet Tan that required a strong work ethic, we'd explain to our new employees that they would be expected to make these kinds of sacrifices. If they wanted to get ahead and be handsomely rewarded at Planet Tan, team members realized they'd have to give up something today for the chance at getting something much better tomorrow.

Newer hires would see how the rest of the team was progressing and being rewarded and they'd think, "Hey, I want that!" So we'd make sure that they understood they could achieve the same rewards, but they would be expected to make the same sacrifices, too. "What are you going to give up to get that?" we'd ask. We'd explain that they'd be giving up their free time; they'd be working long hours; and they'd have to sacrifice partying with their friends or spending time with their families. It's all a trade-off, but if you're willing to invest in your future and sacrifice short-term pleasure, then you'll end up in the right place.

Because it was part of our corporate culture from the top down, our team members understood the concept of sacrifice — they saw it modeled every day. They knew they'd be required to do a whole lot more than just show up and put in the hours. Our staff would have to really be focused, engaged, and committed to constant improvement. They would be asked to stretch beyond their comfort zones — they'd need to be willing to "bring a blanket." They'd be expected to study and to grow personally and professionally. And at the end of the process, those who were willing to make those sacrifices were the ones who would go the farthest at Planet Tan. Any way you slice it, without sacrifice there is no reward.

Tip 35

PAY ATTENTION TO THE PARETO PRINCIPLE

Focus 90 percent of your time on solutions and
only 10 percent of your time on problems.
—Anthony J. D'Angelo

Having come from a marketing background, I was always fascinated by the Pareto principle, more commonly known as the 80-20 rule. The principle suggests that 80 percent of the effects generally come from 20 percent of the causes. One common example is the rule of thumb that 80 percent of your sales come from 20 percent of your customers. This well-known principle was first suggested by business-management thinker Joseph Juran, who named the law after Italian economist Vilfredo Pareto.

Part of the job of every leader is to eliminate distractions and try to channel everyone to focus on a few things that are key to success. In the case of Planet Tan, we used the Pareto principle in our research and analysis to better determine where the company should focus. Keeping an eye on the "law of disproportion" helped us to channel our resources to the appropriate areas. We really were able to see that 80 percent of our problems were coming from a minority of areas. Once we started analyzing our data, we began to find the 20 percent of issues that were causing most of our problems.

We used technology to identify these problem areas by creating exception reports like those I mentioned before. Those reports helped us isolate specific issues. For example, by reviewing the data in the exception reports, we could determine if sales were consistently lower at a particular location, or if problems were occurring at a specific time of day. By peeling back these layers, we were able to identify that 20 percent of the issues may have a significant impact on the business, but if we handled them properly, we could impact 80 percent of our results in the area of focus.

By the same token, we could use our exception reports to see if the majority of positive member reviews were coming in from a particular location, or if the positive comments were attributable to a specific team member. That way, we could recognize and reward our team appropriately. Problems and strengths in an organization are rarely evenly distributed, so keeping the Pareto principle in mind helps you focus on the appropriate areas without becoming too distracted.

Tip 36

A HEALTHY DOSE OF FEAR IS GOOD MEDICINE

Courage is one step ahead of fear.
— *Coleman Young*

Perhaps you've heard the expression, "What would you be or do if you knew it was impossible to fail?" Imagine having the self-confidence to know that your success was inevitable. That's powerful motivation.

By the same token, fear can also be a compelling motivator. Fear of failure can really keep you on your toes. It's one thing to be an employee or to have a job you can quit or walk away from, but it's another story if you *are* your business. Knowing that everything you've got is tied up in your business can be scary, but that fear can also translate into intense focus and proactive management—in other words, good medicine.

Scientists have determined that when we are hungry, our senses are sharpened: We see clearer, hear more acutely, and smell more intensely. It's really not hard to figure out why: This is the body's evolutionary adaptation for survival. When you start getting hungry, your senses begin to home in on what you need to do to find or catch something to eat. In the same way, a little bit of constructive fear can help you gain clarity on what you need to do to make your business successful.

Chances are, if you are an employee working for someone else, you're not totally consumed by your job. When I started my business, though, the one thing that I quickly realized—or maybe it's more accurate to say, became obsessed by—was all the different issues going on in my company. In a start-up, at the very beginning stage of your company, you more than likely have not had time to build a team of people to help you address each and every issue. The biggest reason is that a team like that costs money, which most start-ups lack. So each and every detail of the company must be, in some way or another, touched or overseen by the entrepreneur running the company. This is not all bad news—at least for a while—because it allows you to learn so many vital details that are critical to the success of the business. And, because I had that small dose of fear motivating me, I was more than willing to spend as much time as it took to take care of all the details.

It took me a long time to make the transition, once my company hit a certain level of revenue and results, to hiring people who could give 100 percent of their focus to a specific area of the business. I think I could have done a better job of adding these people sooner, but I was always acutely aware of the costs, so I suppose this was sort of a mixed blessing, though I think it restricted our growth for a period of time.

Another challenge to watch for with the fear motivation is turning it off when you get home. I can honestly say that I had trouble with this for the first ten years of the business; there always seemed to be another issue coming up that needed to be addressed. As I think about it, I'm not sure that I ever really figured it out . . . maybe getting older helped. Eventually, I learned that I could do nothing about the issues by lying awake at night; eventually having other people on the team whom I trusted allowed me to delegate much better.

Having said all that, however, the fear you have when you're starting out, if properly channeled, can keep you on your toes; it can help you stay a few moves ahead of your competitors or inspire you to make internal changes that will spur your business forward. I think this fear—or intensity, or passionate focus, or whatever other label you give it—can be healthy as long as you have other outlets to allow you to blow off steam. I'm not talking about eating or drinking to excess, but rather things that will benefit your mind and body. For some it may be religious faith or meditation.

For me, it was working out five days a week. I always looked forward to my gym time; I could channel my intensity into running or the weight room. The funny thing is that I believe I came up with some of my best ideas for the business during that time! In fact, if you are the one responsible for your own company and your own fate, it means that the enterprise probably occupies most of your waking thoughts. You're committed and you're on the hook for everything. There's no going back; you either make it work or it doesn't work.

When I started Planet Tan, I had just enough fear to push me forward: My reputation was at stake; my finances and my future were on the line; employees and family were depending on me. And I had more than myself and my team members to think about: My mom was counting on me to take care of her once she retired. It was my mom and me on the life raft: If I went down, we both went down. Yes, that healthy dose of fear was a great motivator.

Most of us learned in history classes about how Cortez, upon landing with his army on the shores of the New World, immediately burned his ships. With the ships destroyed, he and his men had no retreat. Surrender was not an option; they had to either be victorious or die. Do you think he and his army were motivated to win the battle?

I felt the same way when I started Planet Tan. Everything—and I mean everything—was wrapped up in my business. If it didn't work, there was nowhere else to go. I had burned my ships back at the shore and had no choice but to charge ahead. I was willing to do whatever it would take to make my business work, because I had that motivational fear of failure.

Tip 37

FIND THE RIGHT THINGS TO DO, THEN DO THEM

Genius is initiative on fire.
— *Holbrook Jackson*

Find the right things to do, then do them. Sounds simple enough, right? If only it were that easy! So many people talk about how incredibly busy they are, yet so often nothing seems to really get done. People frequently confuse activity with accomplishment. You've got to determine the *right* things to do, and then execute. It's about strategy and implementation; neither one is much good without the other.

When I first started out, I didn't order fancy business cards, and aside from moving a tanning bed out of one of the tanning rooms and replacing it with a table and a file cabinet, I didn't spend any time setting up an office. I set my laptop on the table and I hit the ground running. I had decided to focus on the top priorities — designing a winning product and a killer selling strategy — and then dive in and get the job done.

When I founded Planet Tan in 1995, there were 17,000 individual tanning salons and it was a $5 billion industry. That's *billion* with a *B*! I saw an opportunity. I was convinced the tanning business was a sleeping giant that could have great potential if some sound business practices were applied.

At the time, no one in the tanning industry was finding the right things that needed to be done. The business was fragmented and unsophisticated. There was no brand consistency; there were no regional chains or distinctive stores. There was certainly nothing like a Blockbuster or Starbucks in the industry. I realized that a big-box or retail model could be applied to this nascent business. This realization became my game-changing product idea. Despite the public's negative perception of the tanning industry, I realized there weren't any players looking at a more innovative way to run the business. I came in and took a different approach. I was asking myself, "How would Richard Branson of Virgin Records and Virgin Atlantic Airways approach this?" or "How would Jack Welch at General Electric come at this industry?" We had a big-picture, big-brand mentality from the start.

I learned quickly that the industry provided good margins, but the customer experience wasn't great. Much of the business consisted of a couple of tanning beds in the back room of a hair salon or video store. It was an à la carte business where you paid by the session. To me, it looked like an industry in search of a winning business model. That realization led me to develop our innovative sales strategy: creating and marketing an over-the-top, world-class experience for customers.

We applied a membership approach, similar to a health club model. It was a transparent system that was easy to understand: a monthly membership that provided unlimited tanning. Our model was easier to package and easier to market. Ultimately, our model was designed to provide our members with flexibility, convenience, and value. We figured out the right thing to do, then we did it.

We eventually began selling memberships at $19.88 per month for unlimited tanning. This was a great value proposition, because most salons were charging $10 or more per tanning session. We offered an affordable luxury, and with our focus on providing a magical member experience, Planet Tan was also an "escape." A tanning session at Planet Tan was like a twenty-minute vacation. You could get away from the world in a comfortable, pleasing, and fun environment, and you would leave with a healthy glow. We wanted to make people feel better.

We started with three locations, and in the first year we were profitable. None of this success would have been possible without finding the right things to do and then doing them. For Planet Tan, this meant changing the business model and marketing the industry in a whole new way. We created a unique customer experience that was unlike anything they had seen in a tanning salon. We provided consistency and a brand that delivered on our promise.

MAINTAIN A TENACIOUS DESIRE TO SUCCEED

*The history of the world is full of men who rose
to leadership by sheer force of self-confidence,
bravery, and tenacity.*
— *Mahatma Gandhi*

Persistence and tenacity go hand in hand. I attribute much of my success to my sheer tenacity. As far back as I can remember, I was always driven to succeed. Call it traditional Midwestern values, but it's just the way I was raised: You push yourself; you keep going; you finish what you start; and you do what you say you're going to do.

You often hear top athletes described as tenacious, but it goes for business as well—especially when you're trying to launch something that nobody else has ever attempted. When I want something, I go after it with a relentless determination.

One example of persistence paying off is how I was able to hire talent that others in my position might have thought was out of reach. Although I had a small company with just three locations in Dallas when I was first starting out, I immediately went after big-name, national talent for my team.

I recruited the top advertising and marketing executives, the best copywriters, nationally known graphic artists, and even world-renowned architects to design our new stores once we began building them. How did I manage to convince New York ad execs and famous designers to work for our small company? Simply by never taking no for an answer: with pure persistence and tenacity. If I wanted someone to work on my team, I went out and got them. Simple as that. You would be surprised at how many things you can get done just by picking up the phone and asking. The worst thing that can happen is for them to say "no," but you first have to try.

This wasn't just some kind of stubborn or ego-building wild goose chase, either; I realized that for Planet Tan to be successful, I would need to surround myself with the best and brightest people out there—people who shared my belief in persistence and a never-say-die effort. Through tenacity and salesmanship, I was able to make believers out of some big-name talent—so they joined us on our journey.

That same drive and determination helped us land major deals and strategic partnerships—first with the Dallas Stars, and later with the Mavericks and the Cowboys Cheerleaders. Being associated with great promotional partners like these sports teams helped put us on the map in a big way. As a result, Planet Tan looked like a major player—and became one! We were just a local company, but as I've said, we looked to everyone like a national brand. All of this came together because we maintained a tenacious desire to succeed and refused to give up just because we were "only" a local business.

I always saw the benefit of being tenacious; how, through unmitigated desire to achieve, someone could take a losing situation and create success. I recall that at one point we had a location that was declining in sales over time. On the surface, it was easy to blame it on the surrounding area, which had declined over the years. What had once been a thriving neighborhood was beginning to see the effects of time and not enough attention to maintenance.

However, at the location we had a fantastic assistant manager named Robyn who, prior to working for us, had been a stay-at-home mom. Robyn enjoyed getting out of the house and keeping her mind sharp through connecting with people. We really wanted Robyn to go into a store manager position, but we knew it would require more hours and that Robyn was hesitant because of her family responsibilities.

However, she finally agreed to give it a try. As it turned out, Robyn could be one seriously focused gal when she wanted to be, and the fact that this location was our "problem store" was just the challenge she needed to rise to the occasion. We weren't sure exactly what her strategy to turn around the location would be. We discussed a few things, but we ultimately decided to leave it to Robyn and to support her and her team when she wanted our help.

Robyn jumped into management with both feet. The first thing she did after welcoming everyone to the "new team" was to inform them that the store would be the leader in one particular category in thirty days, and then would top another category in the next thirty days! Her sound reasoning was that this effort would create team pride and immediate success. She wanted her store to first win the "Diamond Award," a monthly trophy that moved from one location to the next every thirty days. The Diamond Award was given to the store with the most "sparkle," as rated by the district manager. This was also another way for us to celebrate clean stores.

Robyn had her team pulling all-nighters, and they had the location looking absolutely beautiful. Pictures of the staff went up in the break room, accompanied by captions that told how long each team member had been with the company.

It doesn't take a rocket scientist to figure out that a certain type of person is required to motivate a group of people to not only stay up all night cleaning a store but also be happy to show up—to be excited about being there. Remember also that Robyn had two small kids and a husband at home. But you should have seen the team the next day! They were exhausted, but they had huge smiles on their faces. Plus, the store looked amazing.

I had heard what was going on and made a point to show up the next morning to see what the place looked like. There were balloons, decorations, pictures . . . and the place fairly sizzled with team pride. Robyn's store went on to win the Diamond Award that month, and the very next month they captured Top Sales honors. In fact, they went on to win Top Sales seven out of the next twelve months!

How in the world could this happen in a "rough" area: How could Robyn's store go from worst to first? I'll tell you how: by having one tenacious leader! We went on to name an award in Robyn's honor to capture for the company her spirit and attitude. Robyn knew what we wanted all our team members to learn: Success is tied more directly to what you do and how you think rather than what is going on in the economy or what the world thinks about you. Robyn saw what needed to be done, and even more importantly, she followed through and did it. Her tenacity made her an incredible champion!

Key Insights on the Importance of Persistence

- Is your company saddled by poor-performing employees: Clock-watchers, Cave-dwellers, and Can-kickers? What can you do to lead by example and discourage this kind of attitude? What sacrifices are you willing to make to increase your company's productivity? Have you ever been in the position when you needed to "bring a blanket" to the office?

- Are you a details person or a big picture person? How does that affect your company? Do you have a good balance of strengths on your team? What is your core business? Do you stray from it with "starburster" distractions? Think about ways to expand your business while staying true to the core purpose and mission that you have established. How can you "keep the Main Thing the Main Thing"?

- What are the five main elements of Kaizen? Is your company on a constant quest for improvement? If so, how did you create this environment? If not, what can you do to encourage and motivate your team?

- What are KPIs? Does your company make up-to-date data readily available to employees? How could this foster an atmosphere of friendly competition? What motivation would this have on the top, middle, and low performers?

- What does the Net Promoter Score measure? Could your company benefit from using it? Why or why not? What is the "ultimate question," according to NPS? What is a good NPS score? Remember that important information comes from detractors because they identify areas for improvement.

- What are the three Rs for creating a sustainable business? What is one example of a "game changer" mentality? How can a small company emulate big corporations like General Electric or Nike? What is the advantage of looking at Fortune 500 companies versus the store down the street?

- What is the Pareto principle? How can you use it to understand your business better?

- What are the advantages of implementing exception reports?

- When you are running your own business, fear of failure is magnified on a personal and financial level. You're not just an employee—you are the company, and your fate is tied to it. How can you use the presence of fear as motivation for success?

CHAPTER 5

PROCESS

Building a good business is a process. It starts with selecting the right people, and every decision along the way is just as important as the previous one. A successful company consistently makes smart choices, whether big or small. After reading this chapter, you will understand how to evaluate daily decisions for the betterment of your company, maximize customer service, and continually improve routine business processes. Whether you realize it or not, processes such as how you release employees and accounting and payroll procedures are crucial to the success of your business.

Tip 39

CREATE A "10" MEMBER EXPERIENCE

Great retailers recognize that they're in the business of
constantly surprising and delighting their customers.
— Howard Schultz

One of the biggest reasons for Planet Tan's incredible success was that we focused on creating a "10" member experience. Every single aspect — every minute detail — of the guest's visit to Planet Tan was designed to create that unique, special experience. The entire Planet

Tan experience, from our guests arriving at the parking lot to walking out the door, had to be perfect.

Much of our philosophy about the member experience was modeled after Starbucks and their internal company manual, "The Green Apron." But a truly customer-centric focus can be applied to any business if you're willing to commit to superb member service. In our case, this started with access. Most tanning salons based operating hours on when it was convenient or cost-efficient for the salon to staff them. Planet Tan's operating hours were based on what was convenient for the member. As a result, we were open from 7:00 AM to 11:00 PM, seven days a week. That's 112 hours per week! Nobody else in the industry was open that many hours per week at that time. But we were focused on access and on what would make a "10" member experience, and having convenient hours for our members was our priority. I'll talk more about our focus on access a bit later.

Providing superior access also meant that members should not ever have to wait for a tanning bed. Most salons might have six or seven beds, and some had as many as twelve, which by industry standards was a large facility for the time. By contrast, we averaged about fifty beds per facility. That was a game changer: no waiting! Guests could come right in and have immediate access to tanning. Also, we were consistent and reliable, seven days a week. It didn't matter if one of our guests arrived on a Wednesday afternoon or on a Sunday morning; the experience was always the same, and it was consistently positive.

A lot of little details and nuances added up to a "10" experience for our guests: having two restrooms at every facility; letting our guests choose from six different genres of music in the tanning rooms; providing nice towels on each bed; and maintaining spotless tanning rooms and ultraclean beds. We also had three computers at every location to enable members to check in quickly without having to wait in line.

I mentioned our clean beds: We took a cue from the hotel industry and hired bed cleaners to make sure that the tanning beds were clean and fresh for every new guest. Rather than having the person at the front desk run back and towel off the tanning bed after the member left, we actually had team members who were responsible for making sure those rooms and beds were spotless—right down to folding the high-quality Planet Tan towels we used. Cleanliness was very important to our members, so we made sure that we had the cleanest facilities every time.

In order to create a "10" experience, you've got to put the client's needs before your own. Yes, it will be more difficult, and yes, it will cost you more—but it's also what will give you a unique advantage over the competition. For example, we took such great care of our members that they would abandon their old tanning salons and join Planet Tan. Simply put, we offered a much better value proposition. Guests coming to our facilities knew that they could get longer, more convenient hours; little, if any, wait; new, clean equipment; and professional staff, all for less money than the competition. The member won, and so did we.

THE "10" MEMBER EXPERIENCE

In order to communicate the importance of the "10" member experience to our team, we came up with various themes. We had to make sure our team members understood two things that were vital to the success of the company: return of a member and member referrals. If the customer didn't come back and use the store, we knew we didn't have a chance of getting that member to stay with us over time or to refer us to their friends. However, if we made their visit a "10" experience, there was a much better chance that the member would return and refer.

We created the "EXPERIENCE" acronym to communicate these values to our team:

Everything matters: Retail is in the details. From the clean, well-lit parking lot and the extended hours to the sparkling store windows and the music in our stores, every detail is an opportunity for us to exceed our members' expectations.

Xtraordinary service: We go above and beyond. And even when something goes wrong, a team member goes above and beyond to make things right. These are the experiences our members and guests remember and talk about.

Personable: We are welcoming. We greet each and every one of our members. We want to be a familiar place and treat each member as if he or she has been with us for years. From the moment members walk in to the moment they leave, we want them to feel and know that we genuinely care. Smile and the world smiles back.

Escape: We provide a vacation on every visit. The room represents the member's personal oasis, a chance to get away and relax. Everything needs to be perfect in the room so that nothing can ruin the vacation. We are escape artists.

Responsible: Accountability. It starts with me. I can make a difference. We understand that we are in the business of making people feel better and that each encounter with us needs to be positive. It begins with a great attitude, regardless of outside distractions.

Irresistible: We are not content to be merely liked; we want to be loved. Not the romantic type of love or the love a mother has for a child; instead, we want our members to say, "I love that company."

Experience: We are a learning organization and you are the tanning expert. Use your knowledge to suggest the best path for our members to achieve the best results.

Next step: Create the "next step." From saying, "See you tomorrow," and creating tanning prescriptions, to offering a free trial membership and setting a time the next day or the following that you will see the member, never let a member or guest leave without an opportunity to come back. We may never see them again, and that would make us sad.

Connection: We know our members. Ask questions and pay attention, not just to what they say but how they say it. Only by discovering our members' unique needs can we satisfy them.

Energy: Fun is contagious. When we have fun and feel positive about what we do, we generate positive energy. That energy is reflected on our members and guests and their experience.

Tip 40

GET IN THE TRENCHES

A man can be as great as he wants to be. If you believe in yourself and have the courage, the determination, the dedication, the competitive drive, and if you are willing to sacrifice the little things in life and pay the price for the things that are worthwhile, it can be done.
— *Vince Lombardi*

As an entrepreneur who is likely bootstrapping your own business, you already know that it's not enough to come up with the idea or the financing and let others execute. You've got to be in the trenches, fighting from the foxholes and on the front lines of your business. When I started Planet Tan, I had no illusions about sitting in a corner office and letting subordinates run the show. I knew it would mean working ridiculous hours and being completely immersed in the business. I was totally fine with that notion because I understood that it came with the territory.

No matter how big your dreams and visions, you've got to start in the trenches. For me, this was more than a work ethic and a philosophy—it was a reality and a necessity. Lots of grunt work had to be done, and initially, only a few employees and I were around to take care of everything. One benefit of being in the trenches was that I could lead by example. The staff developed more loyalty because they knew I would never ask them to do anything that I wasn't also doing myself—or hadn't already done.

In the early stages of building the company, we employed a lot of guerrilla-marketing techniques and grassroots efforts. At first, we'd print flyers and then go out into the local community and meet other business owners who were in the same vicinity as our locations. We'd introduce ourselves to people, hand them some flyers, and then give them some free tanning passes. It was a low-cost, high-touch way to introduce Planet Tan to the community.

Another early guerrilla-marketing technique was distributing our flyers on the windshields of cars parked at nearby health clubs or businesses. This isn't the most popular or politically correct way to market today, but at the time we did what we needed to do to promote the business at very little cost. Part of the team members' regular duties included "flyering" cars for a couple of hours every day. Each day, we'd come up with a hit list of which businesses we'd target to distribute our flyers. And every day, we'd get a few new customers who would come in because they saw the flyers. I called these "self-sufficient, gross-producing activities," because if we could generate people walking in the door, we had a chance of converting some of them to members.

The lifeblood of our company in those early days was this type of guerrilla-marketing effort—all those roll-up-your-sleeves sorts of things that could produce traffic to the stores at little or no cost. Long before the Planet Tan brand became hip and sexy, we were in the trenches doing the physical labor. It was sheer motivation and hard work, but we had the attitude that we were building something worthwhile.

Especially in the early days of the company, I was like a street preacher with my staff, and I was right there in the trenches with them. I don't think you can inspire loyalty and motivation if you're calling in from the Bahamas while the staff is on the front lines of the business. You've got to be in there with them. If you're willing to work longer and harder than anyone else, that work ethic will permeate the entire team.

This is particularly important when times are tough or you're in the midst of a critical situation. In times of crisis, it's important to be even more visible and accessible, and to communicate more often. If there's an intense inflection point in your business, then you really need to be available to the troops.

Of course, to begin with, you've got to hire bright, driven, and committed (BDC) staff, and you've got to be a BDC type yourself.

That means you've got to be self-motivated, disciplined, and diligent. You've got to be willing to get up early and to stay late, and you've got to be prepared to do it seven days a week. That commitment and willingness to fight it out in the trenches is a key ingredient for success.

Does this mean you can't be successful if you're always working 24/7? Quite the contrary. Once you've got the right people and processes in place and the business has achieved a certain amount of stability, you can and should enjoy some time off. Freedom and flexibility are important to most entrepreneurs, and taking a break from the business when appropriate can help you avoid burnout, as well as allow you to enjoy the fruits of success.

Tip 41

CHOOSE RIGHT OVER COMFORTABLE

Be willing to make decisions. That's the most important
quality in a good leader.
— *General George S. Patton*

No one likes conflict, and most people will go to great lengths to avoid it. But running a successful business requires making tough decisions, and that's often uncomfortable. Our philosophy at Planet Tan was that you can be comfortable, or you can be right. In other words, you can either do what is comfortable at that moment—knowing deep inside that you're going to pay for that decision later—or you can do the right thing from the start. Doing the right thing creates energy and momentum. This is closely related to following your inner compass, a concept that I'll explain more fully a bit later.

In certain situations, you've got to make a conscious decision to do the right thing, even though that's more than likely *not* the path of least resistance. This is where the "comfortable versus right" choice must be made. The popular decision or the easy decision is not necessarily the right decision.

We adopted this philosophy from our COO, Nick, who had used a similar decision-making process when he had been COO at a major restaurant chain. Nick further distinguishes between comfortable decisions and right decisions: "Comfortable decisions create incremental degradation that kills an organization in small, seemingly unnoticeable chunks, until one day it is too late. It's much like taking a tiny drop of arsenic each morning, which in itself would be uneventful, but will eventually kill a human being. Right decisions create a firm foundation of trust, deep belief in core values, and loyalty for all the correct reasons. Simply making the right decisions consistently raises the bar for everyone, because it becomes expected and indeed demanded, weeding out the impostors."

COMFORTABLE VS. RIGHT

Leaders must constantly make decisions, and it is this multitude of decisions that over time sets the path for success or failure of an enterprise, a relationship, or a career. All decisions are ultimately divided into two defining categories: comfortable or right.

The comfortable decision may be popular and cause momentary good feelings, but it focuses on the short term in a "get through the day without ruffling anyone's feathers" mind-set. The right decision comes from the long-term, strategic perspective that overrides short-term unpopularity in favor of doing what needs to be done for the good of the organization.

Life is a series of small decisions, and even the seemingly minor details—when not handled properly—can slowly derail your business. You compromise here, you let something slide there, and before you know it, you're dying the death of a thousand cuts.

Most businesses that fail do so one bad decision at a time. I used to illustrate this point with my team by using a simple piece of paper. I'd hold up the sheet of paper to represent the company. Then I'd talk about a small problem or bad decision and tear off a little edge of the paper. I'd mention another bad decision, and I'd tear off another piece, then another, and another. Before long there was nothing left of the sheet of paper.

Comfortable versus right is deciding what to tolerate or when to compromise. Your intuition is usually the best guide for this decision. Usually, deep down you know what you *should* do. You've got a gut feeling about the decision you should make. Almost 100 percent of the time, it comes down to either deciding to do the right thing or giving in to doing the convenient thing. These little decisions can have a significant long-term impact. It may seem insignificant now, but too many compromises will eat away at your business.

Let's say, for example, that I had an employee who was a great salesperson, but he was consistently late for his shift. I could let it slide, or I could address the issue. Of course, the right thing to do would be to tackle the problem with the employee, even if he is pulling in good numbers. Turning a blind eye to the situation would be like tearing off one more little piece of that paper.

Worse yet, inaction would quietly communicate to the rest of the team that it's okay for them to not honor their commitment as long as they're reaching their goals. You would be signaling that you've got different rules for different people. That would send the wrong message to your team, and they would become resentful and demoralized. The last thing you want is to be held hostage by one "star" employee.

If I were to address the employee problem, I would have to determine one of three reasons why the employee is always late for work: he doesn't know, he doesn't care, or he can't do. "Doesn't know" can be fixed; "doesn't care" is a sign of a much bigger problem; and "can't do" may just be a logistical or physical problem that can't be rectified. Once you figure out the root of the problem, you again must make a comfortable-versus-right decision.

Chances are, you make dozens of little comfortable-versus-right decisions every day without even giving them much thought. For example, when you show up at the office, what's the first thing you do? Do you take on the most difficult or most important task first?

I would always force myself to do the hardest thing first—to "eat the toad," as the popular business saying goes—even if it wasn't the most convenient. Those are the small decisions that make a big difference over time. Success in business, much like football, is a matter of inches. Each comfortable-versus-right decision you make inches you closer to either success . . . or failure.

Tip 42

DEVELOP YOUR TEAM

Teamwork is the ability to work together toward
a common vision. The ability to direct individual
accomplishments toward organizational objectives.
It is the fuel that allows common people to attain
uncommon results.
—Andrew Carnegie

Since you already know that I believe people are paramount to success, it probably won't surprise you to learn that I also believe that building your team is the most crucial ingredient for your success. No matter how hard you work or how many hours you put in, you can't accomplish big things without the help, support, energy, and expertise of your team. You've no doubt heard the expression that you're only as successful as the five people you spend the most time with—and that certainly applies when it comes to your inner circle or management team.

My primary areas of focus at Planet Tan were marketing, operations, finance, and strategy. I interacted daily with key people who reported to me in these areas, and we would meet weekly as a team to discuss tactical issues. We also conducted a monthly review together and spent one or two days quarterly, looking at the more broad-brush, strategic issues we felt needed to be addressed. This meeting rhythm allowed me to see what each leader thought were the opportunities and threats, and more important, to learn what their plans were to address the areas of focus.

In each meeting with your key people, you are setting the stage for building trust and respect. These meetings don't need to be a time waster; rather, they can be an opportunity to move the ideas at a much faster pace, along with a healthy amount of debate. Each of these leaders was in charge of an area within Planet Tan, so it was important to know how to structure and carry out a meeting, how to create trust, how to encourage healthy debate, and how to have everyone feeling energized when the meeting ends, instead of feeling their time had been wasted.

I loved these sessions with my key team members. I would also meet one on one with each of them during the week to check in and to foster their development. Sometimes I brought in a consultant to work with individuals to help them grow and improve. Other times I would recommend a class to help them gain more knowledge, or even do something as simple as researching a book and purchasing a copy for the individual.

As a matter of fact, I've long been a huge book fan. For very little money, you can gain great insight and ideas. At one point, I even started a book club and contest: Each person in the office would read a particular book and write a few sentences about it as a summary for the rest of the team. The effort became so competitive that people were reading three books a month; many of them told me afterward they previously hadn't read three books a year.

The point is, so much of leadership requires continued learning; a good leader needs a constant flow of ideas that can translate into energy. The job of the leader is to look for ways to help make his or her team the very best, and much of that quest comes down to developing the people who are working directly with you. They, in turn, take responsibility for developing the people who report to them.

If a team member wanted to attend a seminar or take a program that would benefit the company, Planet Tan would pay 100 percent of the cost. Now, I can hear what some of you are thinking: "But, what if everyone wanted to take a class?" My answer would be: "Fantastic, if it's in an area that would help them perform better for the company." Some may worry that people would abuse the system, but at Planet Tan they didn't. We simply asked for them to pay for the course and, once it was completed, to bring in a copy of the receipt along with any type of certification they had earned, and we would reimburse the cost. Such efforts can contribute to developing your key people into stronger and more confident leaders.

I hope you can see that we went to great lengths to build a world-class team at Planet Tan. I literally scoured the country to find the very best talent. As I've already said, I went after big-name talent with a vengeance: from the best Madison Avenue advertising executives to world-renowned architects. You might think it a bit extreme to recruit "superstar" talent for a relatively small chain of tanning salons, but that's how much importance I placed on developing a winning team.

While we're on the topic of recruiting and developing a winning team, let me tell you how I went about getting world-class partners to help me develop Planet Tan. Back in 1995, I noticed how hot the Crunch Fitness brand had become. These guys had a great franchise and they seemed to be doing everything right. Crunch was cool and happening. They had tremendous appeal, and a lot of celebrities and movers and shakers were members. Even though they were only in New York City at the time, Crunch was the hottest fitness brand in the country. They had innovative and sometimes irreverent market-ing and promotion, and appealed to the same basic demographic that Planet Tan was going after in Dallas.

I befriended the founder of Crunch, Doug Levine. We had several great conversations about marketing and the importance of having a great brand. He suggested I contact some of the agencies that were doing marketing for him. One of these was DDB Needham in New York City. I got in touch with one of the key people behind the Crunch brand, Tom DelMundo. Call it audacity or tenacity or just going after what I wanted, but I asked Tom to work with Planet Tan. Now, think about it: Why would an award-winning, national advertising execu-tive working at a top ad agency in New York want to work with a small chain of tanning salons in Dallas? That's where my tenacity and salesmanship came in. Fortunately, Tom and I shared a passion for good advertising and kick-ass branding. Through sheer persistence and force of will, I convinced Tom to work with us on the Planet Tan brand. That's when the magic really started to happen for us.

Tom DelMundo became the architect of the Planet Tan brand and personality, and with Tom and the rest of the team, we turned the tanning industry on its ear. Once Tom was working on our brand with me, we set out to be fun, hip, and irreverent—a far cry from the image presented by the rest of the indoor tanning industry at the time. We started to create some very cool, clever, in-your-face advertising. We wanted to be able to poke fun at ourselves, but do it in a really cute and smart way, with a bit of attitude. A little later, I'll talk more about the ways that Tom helped us make a bold statement with our advertising and marketing efforts.

I hired the best copywriter from another top agency in New York, and I got an amazing graphic artist who ended up being in charge of all of MTV's youth marketing.

Not long after we had Tom DelMundo working on our advertising, I talked to my friend Doug Levine from Crunch about his architect. The Crunch Fitness locations were the epitome of cool; the architecture was amazing. I was about to have my fourth store built, which would be the first location that we were really building ourselves from the ground up, and I wanted to employ Frank Denner, the guy who had designed Crunch Fitness, New York Health & Racquet Club, and the Kimberly Hotel in New York.

I hired Frank in 1997 to design our fourth location. Suddenly, Planet Tan was beginning to look more like a trendy boutique hotel or a funky, stylish bar than a tanning salon. At about the same time, we started to get involved with sports marketing and put together a big deal with the Dallas Stars hockey team. We started to do some slick, sassy advertising. We were working with the Dallas Stars, and lo and behold, in 1999 the team won the Stanley Cup! Now the Planet Tan Team included not just national talent but also national sports teams. We were associating Planet Tan with winners.

In fact, one of my proudest moments in those early years was when Planet Tan got involved with the Dallas Stars. In a major promotion with them, we handed out 18,000 towels with our logo on them at the

Stanley Cup Finals in Dallas. You can imagine the rush of excitement I felt as those thousands of screaming fans were going crazy waving around Planet Tan towels! At the Stanley Cup Championship series!

The lesson here is to surround yourself with the best and brightest people possible to help you achieve your goals. Don't settle for average. Remember that developing your team is much more than just hiring warm bodies to do the work. It's getting the very best talent and allowing them to share and contribute to your collective success. It's creating the right team to build your brand. It's thinking big . . . even when you've only got three locations. That's how you win.

Tip 43

SHARE WHAT YOU KNOW

Real generosity toward the future lies
in giving all to the present.
—Albert Camus

One of the important practices we put into place early on at Planet Tan was the philosophy of having our team members share what they knew—both with each other and with our visitors and guests. We trained our staff to be experts in tanning, and we encouraged them to be generous in sharing their knowledge with our clients.

Everyone on our team understood that we weren't in the tanning business; we were in the business of making people feel better about themselves. That meant we worked to develop personal relationships with our members—to share our knowledge, to be thoughtful, and to genuinely care about our members. Otherwise, we'd end up a transaction-based business and would be no different from the competing tanning salon down the road. Ours was really a *relationship* business.

"Share what you know" was not limited to having our team share their expertise with our members; it was also an important philosophy when it came to sharing and communicating company priorities. One example of how we communicated our priorities was through our frequent managers meetings.

Meetings with your team provide opportunities to obtain multiple ideas from managers who share common values, but different perspectives about how to put those values into practice. Each manager would bring to the meeting his or her own knowledge and experiences, and this variety of perspective, fused by a common purpose, was one of our greatest leadership assets.

I remember that we had one particular issue regarding member service, and each manager, while clearly engaging with the issue, had a unique take on it. The issue had to do with members wanting to use the club while their membership was on hold. Some of the managers wanted to allow the member to use the facilities at a discounted rate, while others thought if they wanted to use the facility then they needed to activate their membership. The problem was common, and by listening to the different views expressed by the managers, we came up with several good alternatives to use in solving the problem.

After lengthy discussion of the pros and cons, the team was collectively able to agree on a fee that was fair to the member, but that did not require complete reactivation. This encouraged the member who wanted to use the facility only a few times, who would be gone most of the time and thus was hesitant to spring for the full, active membership. Our decision was also good for the company, because it generated extra revenue that otherwise would not have come into the stores. As it happened, the idea for the adjusted fee structure came from one of the managers who had given deep consideration about how we could create an opportunity from a situation that at the moment was viewed as negative. If we hadn't had that particular manager engaged enough to put forth a unique solution—instead of just saying, "Well, this is the policy, so here is what I have to do"—we came up with an improvement for a policy that was previously broken. And it all came about because we took the time to assemble a team made up of people willing to share what they knew.

CHECK YOUR EGO AT THE DOOR

Egotism is the anesthetic that dulls
the pain of stupidity.
— *Frank Leahy*

Sharing what you know and giving your best effort to the collective effort works best — especially in small businesses — when there are no egos involved. That may sound like a tall order, especially for people with the chutzpah to stake everything on starting their own businesses, but you've got to make sure that your team members (and you!) leave your egos at the door. Our marketing motto to our members may have been "Feed Your Ego," but that never applied to our team members, especially in our dealings with each other.

Most companies have a traditional, pyramid-shaped organizational chart. As the company grows, there are more and more layers of organization, and the CEO gets further and further away from the foot soldiers at the bottom of the chart. At Planet Tan, I turned the typical organizational chart upside down. The team members were at the top, and I was at the bottom — there to support the rest of the team above me.

We didn't have a lot of layers or levels of middle management. I was never isolated or insulated from the rest of the team. On the contrary, I was always in the thick of things, working alongside the team and pulling my weight with the rest of the staff. As I've said, they knew that I'd never ask them to do anything that I wasn't willing to step up and do myself. We never got too caught up in titles and management structure. Instead, we had a common goal and everyone, at every level, contributed. Egos and attitude didn't enter the mix.

How would it sound if I had called in from some exotic beach while my team was hard at work back at the office? The last thing

I ever wanted to do was to sit up in an ivory tower while the people below me did all the work. I wanted—and needed—to be in the midst of the action, leading by example and setting the standard. Part of my job was to motivate and inspire, and I certainly couldn't do that effectively from anywhere but one of the stores. I was on site and in the fray, with a megaphone in one hand and a stack of cash in the other—doling out equal parts of inspiration and incentives.

It's important to understand this, however: Checking your ego at the door—particularly if you're the boss—does *not* mean being one of the guys or partying with the staff. It's one thing to get in the trenches and work side by side with the team, but that doesn't include going out and getting drunk with your employees or mixing business with pleasure. You've got to maintain the respect of your employees, and dating your employees or partying all night with them will quickly undermine your role as the leader.

Keep in mind that losing your ego means that at some point you will have to display humility. Give credit to those who deserve it. If you make a mistake, be the first to own it. After all, careers last for years, so you're bound to experience both success and failure along the way. Humility in both situations is the hallmark of a great leader.

Tip 45

BUILD SOMETHING TO BELIEVE IN

Live your beliefs and you can turn the world around.
— Henry David Thoreau

When I founded Planet Tan, I wanted it to be a very special place to work. I wanted to create the kind of company where I'd like to work—the kind of place where it would never be "just a job" for team members, but a place where they could develop and thrive and build a career. I wanted to build something to believe in—and that's exactly what we built.

One of the reasons why we had such an exhaustive and highly structured hiring process is because we understood that (here comes the broken record again!) our people *were* the company. At Planet Tan, it all started with the team we put in place. If you made it through the hiring process, the chances were good that you'd soon share our passion for the company. From day one, new team members were indoctrinated into our culture with extensive training and support.

Even our orientation video sent the message loud and clear that Planet Tan was a great place to work — a place where you could really rise through the ranks and make a difference. We worked hard and we played hard. We associated with winners and we sizzled. We realized that we were creating something special together, and we had fun along the way.

As the founder and CEO, I knew I would have to set the tone and get the team in sync to develop this positive culture. Fortunately, I've been called "infectiously enthusiastic," so I had no trouble getting team members to adopt and promote our culture. We created a strong sense of mission and shared common goals. Everyone was rowing in the same direction, and everything we did internally reinforced our mission. From our company rituals to our celebrations and events, everything fueled the belief system and the values we had established for the company.

It wasn't enough just to say that we were building something to believe in; we had to live it. Our mission statement and corporate values were not locked up in a file cabinet somewhere, they were plastered on the walls and in your face — all over our stores. Our team members personified these values with their confidence, pride, and genuine care for our members.

Best of all, there was no disconnect between what we *said* we were building and what you found when you walked in the door. Planet Tan delivered on the brand promise. We more than lived up to the hype; we put our money where our mouth was and over-delivered. That's why our relationships with the sports teams were such a success. It all tied together; it just made sense that Planet Tan was associated with the Dallas Cowboys Cheerleaders, the Dallas Stars, and Mark Cuban and the Mavericks. We were a winner, so we aligned with winners and partnered with the best. We built something to believe in!

Tip 46

ACCEPT RESPONSIBILITY

Responsibility is the price of greatness.
— Winston Churchill

In order to have a team that works together effectively, each team member—and of course, the entire management team—must be accountable. If every member of the staff accepts responsibility for his or her job, that's a good start. However, at Planet Tan, we trained our team to do more than accept responsibility for their particular areas; they had to have each other's backs as well. We went to great lengths to foster an environment where the team was in sync and encouraged to help each other. The only way that you can create a truly remarkable customer experience is if your people are working together for a common goal and they're being held accountable. We trained our team to find the right things to do, and then do them.

If you're going to have that kind of accountability, you've got to give your staff the tools and resources to make decisions and take the initiative. Every team member at Planet Tan was given the authority to take the bull by the horns and tackle any issue they faced. You can't ask for accountability without giving your team members the authority to take action. Accordingly, those at every level of the Planet Tan Team understood that they were responsible for member satisfaction and that they could do anything necessary to serve our guests.

Of course, the boss has got to set the tone and establish the kind of work environment that rewards teamwork and recognizes those who go above and beyond in accepting responsibility. Since accountability starts with the CEO, I set a high standard for myself before expecting it of my team.

I recall that once we had a glitch where we double-charged a client's credit card. Naturally, we fixed the problem, but we had inconvenienced one of our members. To try and make it right, we delivered flowers to the member's office. Who brought her the flowers with a personal apology? Not a messenger, not a staff member, not even the store manager. I, the head of the company, delivered the flowers. If you want your team to follow your instructions, the quickest way to get their attention is to lead by example—in both word and deed.

We always told our team to never let the sun set on a problem, to always address the issue at the earliest possible moment. As mentioned earlier, we called it our "dusk policy"; get back to someone before the end of the day. Don't avoid the problem or put it off, and don't let it wait until tomorrow. We always wanted to resolve issues before they became bigger issues. It's a bit like the old marriage philosophy of never going to bed angry. We set expectations so that potential problems could be addressed and dealt with before the day was over. Not only was it the right thing to do; it also sent a message that we cared, that we were accountable.

Tip 47

PRACTICE COMPASSIONATE TERMINATION

Compassion will cure more sins than condemnation.
— *Henry Ward Beecher*

When someone fails in an organization, it is a burden shared equally by the individual and the organization that they became a part of. Furthermore, the truth is that the opportunity created by terminating someone may ultimately benefit both sides. You are helping that person move on to the next chapter of his life, and chances are he knew (deep down inside), just as you did, that he was struggling. While the good-bye conversation is almost always regrettable, it is *seldom a surprise*.

General George S. Patton said it well: "The wrong guy in the wrong place on the battlefield can cause the death of a hundred good men. My job is to ensure that every son of a bitch that belongs here stays and that anyone else is peeling potatoes in the mess hall where he can't hurt anyone." By stepping up to the responsibility of taking care of this unpleasant aspect of leadership, you are protecting your organization and allowing the individual being terminated to move on to the next opportunity—one that may be more in line with his true abilities.

When separation becomes necessary, take responsibility openly for the role the organization played in the person's failure, and then hold her accountable for her side of the equation. Share what she contributed, and then turn the discussion toward moving on and learning from the experience. Be concise; avoid small talk and comfortable gibberish because, in the final analysis, it's just a shield for your own discomfort and it serves neither party.

While termination is an emotional and life-changing event, it is a necessary function of any organization. As such, the process of letting someone go must be handled as carefully as his first day on the job. Termination is a time for dignity and compassion, blended with steely resolve that comes with the territory of leadership.

Tip 48

KEEP YOUR INFO ONE CLICK AWAY

As a general rule the most successful man in life
is the man who has the best information.
—Benjamin Disraeli

Many entrepreneurs, being creative types or "idea" people, cringe at the notion of research, analysis, and metrics. However, accurate measurements are a critical indicator of the success of a business. After all, what can be measured can be improved, so it's crucial to know your numbers.

The real challenge is determining *which* metrics are key to the success of your business so that your organization is provided the tangible knowledge that best assists you in critical decision making. By contrast, the last thing you need is arbitrary data. Finally, those key metrics have to be delivered in an accurate and timely matter. Stale research doesn't do anyone any good.

At Planet Tan, we developed the strategy of having valuable information just one click away. This strategy involved providing the right information to the right people in the right format so that it required one click of a mouse to access.

For example, every morning our store managers would have a "daily huddle" with their district managers, in which they would review their numbers from the previous day and set a strategy for the current day. That meant taking about ten minutes per day per store to run all the necessary reports and compile the key metrics that our team used in the meeting.

We automated this process so that every morning a new form with the daily huddle format with all the previous day's metrics was waiting on the store's computer when the managers arrived; the information was just one click away. By automating just this one report, we saved at least two-and-a-half labor hours per day.

We also used the one-click-away strategy to drive metrics. Our operations staff would develop contests aimed at improving a particular metric. We were able to automatically provide team members with a "stack rank report" on how everyone was performing on the contest. This scoreboard created a friendly competition among the team members and made it easy to see who was in the lead and who was still in the running.

We also created a "cadence schedule," a scheduled calendar for pushing out information to the appropriate person at a particular time of day on a certain day of the week. We wanted to make sure we strategically communicated information so that the right team members could do something with the information for the better.

Daily sales were posted on the computer for everyone to see and updated every five minutes so that the most current information was on every terminal. In fact, this one piece of data drove everyone's competitive nature: If you were on top of the sales, you wanted to stay there, and if you were on the bottom, you wanted to move up as soon as possible. Again, the idea was to keep the key information easily accessible and at our fingertips.

Once we started the automation process with reporting, the savings in labor hours, the improved efficiency, and the better team member performance were not only significant but also contagious and motivating. Each department began coming up with ways to improve and automate routine tasks they performed. Even the team members who might have initially felt a bit threatened by the idea of automating their job soon embraced it. They realized that automating and streamlining freed them up to focus on the parts of their job that they really enjoyed and gave them more time to take on new challenges. Eventually, our automation efforts and one-click-away strategy became part of the Planet Tan culture.

Automating routine tasks also allowed us to consolidate and streamline many of our processes. One of the best examples came from a team member in our accounting department. She realized she was spending a considerable number of hours per month entering the daily sales numbers from each store into our accounting system. It was a cumbersome process requiring our stores to print out a report template, fill in a spreadsheet, and then send all the information in each week along with their deposit slips and receipts.

After reviewing the process, we decided to create a software application for the stores to enter their drawer counts. All of the numbers that the staff had previously provided manually were now pulled from our point of sale and credit card software, so the team member could just hit the "submit" button to send everything to our accounting department. We received downloads from the bank that we cross-referenced with what the stores had entered, so we could quickly determine if a deposit wasn't made. Then a file was created so that general ledger entries were imported. This process saved about twenty hours per month in accounting, as well as saving fifteen minutes of staff time per day, per store. In addition to producing better tracking and auditing procedures, it also created a scalable process so that we could grow without additional labor. In short, it pays to keep your information one click away!

Tip 49

UTILIZE BUSINESS INTELLIGENCE

If we knew what it was we were doing, it would not
be called research, would it?
—*Albert Einstein*

Closely related to knowing your numbers is ensuring that you're using your business intelligence effectively. Due to government regulations, the tanning industry is required to keep detailed data on all of our members. Every transaction is assigned to a customer, and in our database, we stored each member's age, gender, and address. Fortunately, this government mandate forced Planet Tan to acquire what most companies had to spend time and money trying to get from loyalty programs. By having this depth of data on our members, we were able to mine it and answer many questions. What is the value of a member? Are our memberships priced at the optimal point to generate the most profits while at the same time increasing the lifetime value of a member? Would raising the price for a monthly membership really make a difference? Where should we open our next location? Planet Tan was zealous in our use of research to drive constant improvement.

For example, we developed one study to determine if charging $5 more a month would have an impact on our premier level membership, and if so, to what extent. We had originally offered our premier membership at $19.99 and increased the sale price of new memberships to $24.99 after a few years. We felt that the $24.99 was the right price point, but we wanted to know what effect a 20 percent price increase might have. So we set out to answer a few questions: Did the price difference affect the rate at which people acquired the membership? Did the people at the $24.99 price cancel or put their memberships on hold more often than those at the $19.99 price did? Who spent more money on retail products? Which customer was ultimately more valuable? To answer all of the questions, we selected a month and did a price roll back to $19.99 for half the month. Ironically, we sold almost the exact number of $24.99 versus $19.99 memberships that month. We monitored the members in each price group for more than eighteen months to track how many canceled or went on hold, along with how much they spent on retail products and in total. What we learned was that the $24.99 members spent more each month in retail (with the exception of December), and they canceled by a couple of percentage points more. However, the $24.99 group generated considerably more revenue than their $19.99 counterparts did. Thus, we were able to conclude, on the basis of reliable data, that it made sense to raise the monthly membership rate.

Later we partnered with the Buxton Group, a growth and business strategy company located in Fort Worth, to better identify what customer paradigm our members included. This research included basic demographics in addition to revealing psychographics. We wanted to know more than age and gender; we wanted to study our members' attitudes, beliefs, and behaviors. We wanted to better understand member profiles: Who drives a Volvo? Who subscribes to certain magazines or buys organic food? We determined that there were five or six distinct types of Planet Tan members.

We utilized this information to better target future members and to strategically place our new store locations. Obviously, new store location placement was a key business decision, so we studied this research very carefully. We found out how the big-box stores like Target and Best Buy were selecting locations and using information to help analyze the best chance for success of a new store. We also found out that the Buxton Group specialized in analyzing the profiles of our customers. Based on that information, we could better determine where stores needed to be placed, if there would be any cannibalization of customers from current stores, and what the first-year sales projections for the new locations would look like, based not just on the number of people in the area, but the number of "target customers" who had the propensity to do business with the company.

Over the years, the Buxton Group became another important vendor partnership, helping us decide not only where a new store should be placed but also when we should move a store from an area that had changed. In addition, they helped us form a clear idea of how many stores we would be able to open in a given market.

As with all information, one piece was not the entire puzzle, but the data we began to gather became very critical components in our long-term strategy. By working with Buxton, we were utilizing a very sophisticated and technical process for determining new store locations. We'd analyze the Dallas/Fort Worth Metroplex and look for pockets of people who fit the Planet Tan profile. The location analysis would get right down to the neighborhood and the street.

We also analyzed the timing of a new store opening and discovered that the optimal time to open a store was right at the start of the tanning season. By analyzing our metrics and utilizing our business intelligence, we were able to make more of our locations profitable more quickly. Any business can gain key insights into its current business to better determine ways to make it more successful. The key is not to look at an undifferentiated lump of data, but rather to tease out the details that will help you make your business more compelling. Make the information actionable.

Tip 50

MAKE YOUR VENDORS YOUR PARTNERS

When you're part of a team, you stand up for
your teammates. Your loyalty is to them. You protect
them through good and bad, because they'd
do the same for you.
— Yogi Berra

In some companies, there is an adversarial or tense relationship with the company's vendors or suppliers. That never made sense to me. At Planet Tan, I set out to make our vendors more like our partners. In fact, throughout the history of my business, my key vendors also became my partners as well as my trusted advisers.

Two of my biggest partners were my lotion vendor and my tanning equipment company. The reality was that we sold time in a tanning bed and products that help the skin tan better. One hundred percent of our members would experience these two vendors' products. Because we were loyal to them and viewed these vendors as partners from day one, they extended Planet Tan favorable terms and actually helped to finance the growth of our company.

Turning vendors into partners starts with the Golden Rule, slightly revised: "Do unto your vendors as you would have them do unto you." In other words, treat your vendors the way you want to be treated. If you expect to be paid on time, then pay your suppliers on time.

In addition, we thought that if we were a good partner to our vendors, we could collaborate. Rather than just viewing our vendors as regular suppliers, we developed a relationship where we would be able to share best practices and leverage the brainpower and management experience of these other companies. After all, different industries develop new and different ideas, and we realized that we could learn a lot from each other. Our vendors, in other words, had more to offer us than just the products and supplies we used in our day-to-day operations; they could offer us crucial business intelligence. And we could return the favor.

For instance, from our lotion vendor we were able to learn a great deal about supply chain and apply those best practices to our business. We worked closely with our equipment supplier to evaluate the right "bed mix" for our stores. We were utilizing five different types of tanning beds in our locations, so understanding the best ratio would help us improve our customer service and satisfaction.

On the flip side, we shared ideas and information with our vendors to help improve their products and services. We gave our lotion company access to our members for sampling opportunities and let them use our data to see which lotion products were doing the best. In addition, we gave them access to our team members so they could get even more feedback on their products.

Another great example of working with our vendors for mutual benefit was when we worked with our tanning equipment supplier to innovate new enhancements and features for their tanning beds. In the early days of Planet Tan, when we wanted to provide music in the tanning rooms, we'd have to manufacture everything separately—the speakers, the channel selector, the controls, etc. Working closely with the tanning bed manufacturer, we were able to collaborate on development of the first beds that had all the music elements built into the bed! We were the first tanning company to introduce music not just into the tanning room, but right into the bed! If not for our collaboration and relationship with our vendor/partners, none of this would have been possible. But with collaboration, everybody wins.

Key Insights on Focusing Your Process

- What are a few examples of ways you can surprise and delight your customers? Give big-picture and detail-oriented options. Think about the acrostic for "EXPERIENCE"; which tip is implemented the best at your company? Which tip could you work on?

- Can you think of an example when you did something that was comfortable instead of what was right for your company? How did that decision affect your business? What would you do differently in that situation today? On the flip side, consider a time when you made the right call, even if it meant extra work or an awkward confrontation. How did that turn out in the long run?

- Who are the five people you spend the most time with? How do they influence the way you operate? Having a top-notch staff is an important aspect of any successful business. You are only as strong as your weakest link. Think about actionable steps you can take to associate with people and companies more successful than you. The experience will only make you better.

- What does the organizational chart in your office look like? How would it change your business if you flipped the traditional dynamics and were in the trenches with your employees? What does it mean to check your ego at the door? What doesn't it mean?

- How do you become "A company to believe in"? Where is your business in that process? List several examples of ways to foster an environment of accountability.

- Consider the do's and don'ts of practicing compassionate termination.

- Is your company information "one click away"? What could automating routine tasks mean for your company?

CHAPTER 6

 **PERSONALITY**

It's easy to articulate what makes a good friend: Someone who is honest, loyal, hardworking, and considerate would surely make everyone's list of ideal traits. While it's simple to say, it's harder to live out. Whether in personal or professional relationships, personality counts. In a customer-driven environment, these qualities are paramount. This means ensuring a consistent company personality from the front desk staff to the CEO. This chapter will give you tangible steps to define your company's personality and to utilize positive personality characteristics in designing customer service initiatives and intra-company policies.

Tip 51

GRACE IN ALL SITUATIONS

*Through many dangers, toils and snares, I have already
come; 'Tis grace has brought me safe thus far,
and grace will lead me home.*
—*John Newton*

Maybe it's my Midwestern background, or just the way my mom brought me up, but I've always believed in the value of fairness. I was taught never to take advantage of people, so obviously my company reflected those values. Team members at Planet Tan were trained to be confident, but never arrogant; humble, but not shy; irreverent, but not disrespectful.

Another word for it is grace. We must learn to be more gracious in business. I learned this lesson when I was just twenty-three years old and working in Cedar Rapids, Iowa. I probably thought I was a big deal at the time, being in charge of all these people and all these health clubs. But the owner of the chain was a wise Korean gentleman, and he taught me a few things about grace.

The lesson that resonates the strongest is one he taught me while we were eating dinner in a restaurant. On a napkin he drew a picture of an apple tree. He explained how the apples sticking up on the branch were not ready to eat; when they were heavy and ripe, however, they would hang below the branch. In the same way, he explained, someone who is proud is not ready to lead. He then talked about the large apples. "Notice the branches bending down under their weight," he said. In other words, a good leader has his head down in humility, not held high in pride. Where the branches were bent low (with their "heads" humbly bowed), the apples were ripe and in their prime—the best apples on the tree.

His point was that even when you're in a position of power, you should show some humility and grace. Do not put yourself above others or take advantage of the less powerful. Maintain your gratitude and respect. After all, the tables will be turned at some point, and next time it might not be you in the position of power.

If you take the long view, you'll probably realize that any business relationship may last a long time, so if you show some grace and fairness when you're "up," your loyalty and humility will be rewarded when you're "down." The best leaders know this; they hand out the credit to the team when there's a victory, and when something goes wrong, instead of pointing fingers, they accept responsibility. Having grace in both good and difficult situations is vital to long-term success.

I suppose it's just another take on the Golden Rule. Treating others the way you want to be treated works in business, as in life. The good news is that I've found you can run a successful business and make a sizable profit even if you're a nice guy! For me, fairness and integrity in business were much more than just buzzwords; they were the values we used as the foundation for our company.

Furthermore, how you deal with a situation in difficult times sends a signal to people about how you'll deal with them anytime. It's easy to be all smiles when the sun is shining, but it's maintaining that attitude when things get stormy that matters. Another way of looking at it is the old expression: "How you do anything is how you do everything."

Tip 52

LOYALTY MATTERS

The foundation stones for a balanced success are
honesty, character, integrity, faith, love, and loyalty.
— Zig Ziglar

I'll take someone who is loyal and dependable over someone with more experience any day. Give me a candidate who demonstrates loyalty and has the right attitude, and, I assure you, that person can learn and grow into a particular job. There's no substitute for truly dependable people. You know that their word is good and that they can be counted on. They don't need to be micromanaged, and they give you back your most precious commodity: time.

Employees with much more business experience who may not be as loyal have their own agendas. Without loyalty, it's possible that those employees are always going to be on the lookout for a bigger and better deal. Over the long haul, the less dependable employees—even though they may have more experience—will sap your energy and dampen morale.

Without loyalty and dedication, your organization is a house of cards. Of course, loyalty works both ways: If you expect loyalty from your team, you've got to demonstrate your loyalty to them. One of our key battle cries was "One Planet Tan," meaning that we were all on the same team, going in the same direction.

With our One Planet Tan philosophy, we encouraged consistency in management and messaging. It helped create buy-in for the newer employees and helped us maintain continuity in our culture. Team members shared a positive attitude; they shared an urgency and a common sense of purpose. This wasn't always easy, especially with certain positions such as accounting—positions that are not typically known for their creativity or flexibility.

Loyalty is not necessarily the same as longevity or tenure. Just because you've got employees who have been there for years and are still punching the clock and doing their time, it does not mean that they are loyal or productive. Not unlike with sports teams, in business you can't always keep someone around if they're well past their prime and not contributing anymore. Someone who is loyal, however, will give you their best, whether they're in year one or year twenty.

Tip 53

FOLLOW YOUR INTERNAL COMPASS

There is no such thing as a minor lapse of integrity.
— *Tom Peters*

I've got a big compass on my desk. It's there as a not-so-subtle reminder to follow my internal compass—that gut instinct and intuition that usually keeps us on the right path. It seems to me that the only time we get ourselves into trouble is when we ignore that little voice deep inside each of us. As I've already suggested, we're usually far better off when we listen to our intuition.

After all, most folks know right from wrong. We just need to pay attention to our internal barometers and trust our instincts. Anyone can justify a wrong decision, but it's still a wrong decision. I follow a certain standard of values and do my best to lead by example, not just at work, but throughout my life.

I spoke earlier about the importance of focus and not getting distracted by "starburst" ideas. This is definitely a component of following your internal compass. Likewise, doing what's right instead of what's convenient or easy comes into play here as well.

But staying on course over the long haul involves more and goes deeper. The ability to pay attention to your internal guidance system means you will stay focused on more than business strategy and intent upon more than doing the right things at the right time; it also requires an encompassing sense of what your company is and is not.

There were times in my years at Planet Tan when we were being challenged to go in different directions. Only the internal resolve to stay on course, arising from a constitution of steely resolve based on my belief in my decision, allowed me to stay the course when others were in disagreement, when my decision was not popular and was even being second-guessed.

Stay the course if you truly believe what you are doing will ultimately bring you to your goal. You may not get there as quickly as some would like, and you may choose not to pursue some interesting idea that is being promoted.

However, stay the course, knowing that your internal compass is leading you in the right direction.

BREAK AWAY FROM THE HERD
The landmark 1955 Conformity Experiment by psychologist Solomon Asch studied the effects of group mentality. In the experiment, only one out of nine participants was actually being studied; the rest were actors told to give the same incorrect answer. The participant being studied was never the first to answer and became visibly uncomfortable and disturbed as the actors called out the same incorrect answer. Nevertheless, he stuck to his guns only 29 percent of the time. The other 71 percent of the time, the participant sided with the obviously incorrect majority.

This experiment shows that more often than not, we are willing to go against our own sound judgment in order to fit in with a group. Don't fall victim to a herd mentality in your business. Define your principles and stay the course, no matter what anyone else is doing.

Tip 54

LEARN SOMETHING NEW EVERY DAY

Learning is ever in the freshness of its youth,
even for the old.
—Aeschylus

As I mentioned above, we always made sure that Planet Tan was very much a learning organization. As a lifetime learner myself, I wanted to bring that insatiable hunger for constant improvement to the company. That's why we focused so heavily on learning and professional development. We knew if we could improve and grow just a little bit every day, we'd have a winning organization. But that would never have happened if I hadn't been fundamentally committed to the importance of learning in my own life. As a leader, you have to be a learner. The fact is that the day you decide you have nothing left to learn, you begin to die—and eventually, you'll take your company down with you.

As I've mentioned, we encouraged our team to learn something new every single day, and we provided the environment where they could do that. If you joined the Planet Tan Team, you were held to a higher standard than just showing up and working your shift; you were expected to read books, attend seminars, and complete various training programs.

The primary reason for this corporate and cultural emphasis was my own insatiable appetite for growth and learning. The fact is that you can't lead people unless you know the way yourself. As with all the other principles discussed in this book, a leader who wants his or her people to be learners must set the tone and lead by example. I'm grateful that this was never a problem for me; learning was and is an integral part of who I am. If you want to be the best leader you can possibly be, never stop learning. Read, attend seminars, take classes, talk to mentors and industry leaders—do whatever it takes to keep the ideas and the energy they represent as a constant in your mind and life.

Tip 55

UNLEASH YOUR SELF-CONFIDENCE

*If you have no confidence in self, you are twice defeated
in the race of life. With confidence, you have won
even before you have started.*
— *Marcus Tullius Cicero*

Let's face it: Self-confidence is sexy; it's contagious. Being self-assured makes you feel better about yourself, which can help you make others feel better about themselves. Part of the reason we focused so heavily on training and personal development at Planet Tan was so that our team members would be competent and confident. Competence builds confidence, and we wanted our team members to exude confidence.

At Planet Tan, our employees were never simply front desk staff or receptionists—they were tanning *consultants*. They were groomed and trained to be tanning experts, and we made sure that they lived up to that role. In fact, our team didn't just give tanning advice, we provided tanning *prescriptions* for our guests. Because they had been trained extensively and given the tools to help them shine, our team members were always confident, positive, and self-assured.

This is not only beneficial to the team member, but it also helps to reassure our members and guests and give them confidence in Planet

Tan and what we offered. Our members understood that they could count on the Planet Tan staff to provide them with the best advice and support—along with the best overall member experience.

When you combine a supportive, knowledgeable staff with personality and confidence, you've got a winning combination. When our team members put their own, unique personalities into the mix, it gave Planet Tan a competitive advantage that couldn't be duplicated. Our team cared about our members. They connected with them and did everything possible to make them feel special. None of this would have been possible if our staff did not have that extra measure of confidence in their own abilities.

In all honesty, at the end of the day, most of our competition had the same equipment and access to the same information and resources. What they couldn't match was the "10" member experience provided by our knowledgeable, confident, energetic, and personable team members. Remember, we were not in a transaction-based business; we were providing a relationship-based service.

Working on building the team's competence will translate into confidence and an environment that will bring out the best in people. When your staff is confident, there is energy in the air; they have the tools and attitude to get out there and compete. Your team members will rise to meet new challenges because they believe they can do it. As a leader, you must help them believe they can accomplish more.

Tip 56

ALWAYS BE PERSONABLE

*Lead the life that will make you kindly and friendly
to everyone about you, and you will be surprised
what a happy life you will lead.*
— *Charles M. Schwab*

The tanning business, much like a health club, is typically a transactional industry. However, we wanted to differentiate Planet Tan by focusing instead on relationships. Obviously, one way to do that is to genuinely care about your customers. On a very basic level, this begins by not referring to them as customers. As you may have noticed throughout this book, we always referred to our customers as "members." It's a subtle, but important distinction. A member, by definition, means the person is a part of something, which on a conscious and subconscious level conveys that the person is special, accepted into the fold. We called customers who were not yet members "guests." Depending on the nature of your business, "member" and "guest" may not be the most appropriate terms for your customers; spend some time coming up with words that could help convey to your customers their importance to your organization.

As I've said already, in order to be successful, we knew that we'd have to move beyond a transaction-based business and into a relationship-based model, so we trained our team to be personable and to connect with our members. We hired passionate people with great personalities. Their focus was on our members and on making sure that our members received exceptional service and had a "10" experience every time they visited Planet Tan. We did that by building and developing strong relationships with our members.

At Planet Tan, we realized that we were not so much competing with the tanning salon down the road as we were competing for our member's disposable time. Time was every member's most valuable and precious commodity, so if a member shared her time with us, we should reward her commitment with an amazing experience. We felt it was an honor that people chose to spend time with us, so we wanted to honor them back by making them feel better about themselves.

We offered an escape from the ordinary—a unique and special experience. We fulfilled a basic human need: We made people feel important. We developed personal relationships with our members that went well beyond a transaction. We were personable.

We took time to really take care of our members. Sometimes it was just the little things: making it a point to know and use their names or giving them a sincere compliment. Other times it was a friendly word of encouragement or loaning the member an umbrella if it was raining. Planet Tan provided our members and guests with a caring staff and a sense of belonging and acceptance. In doing so, we turned a traditionally transactional business into a personable, relationship-driven business.

In every business there is a way to come up with regular surprises that create loyalty and excitement in your customers or clients. With technology it's easy now to e-mail personal communication to customers based on dates and specific thresholds of business. The more personal these become, the more connection the customer has with the business. Remember: It's much easier to retain a current customer than to obtain a new one—and much more profitable. Think of ways to make sure the customer cannot live without you—or at least will miss the relationship if he discontinues it.

TAKE A LESSON FROM GENERAL PENCIL

It is no secret that manufacturing products in China is economically advantageous. So why are there even pencils that still say, "Made in America"? Enter General Pencil, a New Jersey–based, family-operated pencil manufacturing company that started in 1889. A century after its founding, the family biz was in trouble. Facing pressure to downsize or close up shop altogether, General Pencil started asking consumers how to better serve the public need for pencils.

The company discovered that while the writing utensils made in China were cheap, they didn't come with the level of personal service and accommodation that General Pencil's products did. General Pencil listened to consumers and adapted to new needs, like those of artists who were in the market for high-quality drawing and sketching pencils. By discontinuing the marketing of No. 2 pencils, General Pencil was able to focus precious time and resources on the high-end merchandise customers weren't getting from China. After a century of pencil-making as usual, it wasn't easy for General Pencil to change and shift gears. But a truly personable business knows how to listen to its customers and find new ways to relate to them.

Key Insights on Leading with Personality

- Why should you show grace to others in business? Explain the apple analogy in your own words. How do you show grace and humility in a business relationship?

- When you interview new employees, what qualities do you look for? Do you consider loyalty and dependability to be more important than experience? How can you gauge these abstract characteristics? Loyalty is a two-way street. What can you do to express your dedication to current employees and build their loyalty to the company?

- Having confident employees puts the customer at ease and makes your business run more efficiently. Have you empowered your employees to be self-confident? If so, how did you do it? If not, what are some ways you could instill confidence in your team?

- Is your business transactional or relational? What are the characteristics of a relational business? How can you better exemplify them? Are your employees personable or merely polite? What's the difference between the two?

CHAPTER 7

POSITIVITY

No matter what type of business you are in, the power of a positive attitude cannot be overstated. Your attitude sets the tone for the rest of the company, and having an optimistic outlook can make all the difference. If you're looking at the glass as half full instead of half empty, it's natural to encourage your team, set goals, and constantly improve. A negative attitude takes the wind out of your sails and detracts from company progress. In this chapter, you will learn how to use a positive attitude to launch significant short- and long-term goals, associate with winners, find great mentors, and learn from your competition.

Tip 57

ALWAYS STAY POSITIVE

Perpetual optimism is a force multiplier.
— *Colin Powell*

In order to be successful, you've got to be self-motivated and you've got to have staying power. Maintaining a positive attitude helps you persevere when things get tough. Despite my challenging childhood, I was always able to keep a positive outlook. I suppose I could have played the victim and felt sorry for myself, but thanks to my upbringing and my mom's great example, I kept my chin up and persevered.

I carried that optimism into my adulthood, and it served me well as I built my company. Creating a winning business with a great culture takes 24/7 energy and enthusiasm, and I've always done my best to set the standard as the tireless, eternal optimist. Staying upbeat was especially important in the early days, as I had to motivate a young team. At the time, Planet Tan was defined by sheer motivation and inspiration. It was just a small group of young, enthusiastic people who believed they could accomplish anything.

I'd keep the team pumped up and excited about our mission. I was the cheerleader and the street preacher, and my gospel was the company; I'd preach the Planet Tan message to anyone who would listen. That energy and optimism fueled our growth and kept us in the game whenever we faced difficult challenges.

As an entrepreneur, you simply cannot underestimate the importance of a positive attitude. It's impossible to be a bootstrapper-type entrepreneur without being energized and being able to energize other people. Furthermore, putting positive, energetic people on your team will improve the team's performance, because the energy will be shared and transferable. You've got to maintain that positive mental attitude, come rain or come shine. Of course, that's where your passion comes in; if you're passionate about what you're doing, it's going to be a lot easier to stay positive when things get rough.

Tip 58

SET BIG GOALS

The victory of success is half won when one gains the habit of setting goals and achieving them. Even the most tedious chore will become endurable as you parade through each day convinced that every task, no matter how menial or boring, brings you closer to fulfilling your dreams.
— Og Mandino

You may have heard the expression "Big, Hairy, Audacious Goals" (BHAGs). As you can possibly guess, I was always a huge proponent of setting audacious and ambitious goals. At Planet Tan, we didn't just talk about goals once or twice a year, we kept them in sight every day. We had individual goals, team goals, and of course, sales goals. We also developed a three-year and a ten-year plan. We mapped out specific, measurable benchmarks and put them on a big diagram and timeline for all of us to share.

We adopted our BHAG philosophy from my friend and colleague Verne Harnish, CEO of a business consulting firm called Gazelles, Inc. We learned the importance of setting far-reaching, long-term goals—the more ambitious, the better.

Each year, the team would agree on a strategy and growth plan to ensure that we hit our numbers and continued to grow the company. Our goals were always on the computers at each store location as well as in the hallway of the corporate office. We also revisited the plan in each monthly meeting so we could evaluate current results against the goals we'd set. All of the plans and visuals were communicated and shared with the team to keep us on track and moving in the same direction.

The team appreciated being able to visualize how the company planned to grow over the next several years. We charted out how many stores we planned to open year by year, as well as specific revenue goals for the company all along the timeline. Our timeline was very detailed, and we followed it to a "t." We mapped out our location remodels, how we'd fold profits back into the business, and when and where we'd open a new store. Every detail was discussed; nothing was left to chance.

Our unique "Six-Part Process for Growth" was another visual representation of our key strategies for growing the business. This diagram listed the six main themes we'd need to focus on each year to drive growth. For us, this was goal setting in action; it was where the concepts became reality, and the chart demonstrated how we'd execute the plan day to day.

In the "Execute for Growth" diagram seen in appendix 1, you can see how we illustrated our plan for growth based on six key themes: Team Members, Innovation, Automation, World Class, New Store Growth/Same Store Growth, and Growth Leaders. Mapping out our annual goals and key initiatives was vitally important to Planet Tan, and it helped us achieve double-digit, organic growth each year.

Of course, you can't confuse activity with accomplishment. Ultimately, you're judged on what you do, not what you say you want to do. You've got to make sure that the success you are creating today creates long-term health for the company over time. For example, anyone can lay people off and not reinvest in the business to boost their numbers in the short-term, but real success comes from a complete dedication to serving your employees, customers, and company all at the same time.

Tip 59

PROVIDE REAL ENCOURAGEMENT

Few things in the world are more powerful than a
positive push. A smile. A word of optimism and hope.
A "you can do it" when things are tough.
— Richard M. DeVos

At the beginning of this book, I talked about my disdain for false flattery and patronizing behavior. However, that doesn't mean you should ever withhold sincere praise or appreciation. As Mary Kay Cosmetics founder Mary Kay Ash once said: "Everyone has an invisible sign hanging from their neck saying, 'Make me feel important.' Never forget this message when working with people."

I also recall the words of author John Dewey, one of America's most profound philosophers, who pointed out that the deepest urge in human nature is the desire to be important. Then, of course, there's Abraham Maslow's famous Hierarchy of Needs, which lists love, belonging, and the need for respect as among some of the most basic human requirements.

Early on, even though we had no budget to speak of, we understood the importance of encouragement, and this became the foundation of our culture. I'm convinced that this was one of the most important aspects of Planet Tan's success. It was very natural to me to want to see the people around me succeed. I always enjoyed encouraging my team to grow and thrive. We developed a culture of mutual support where everyone was generous in their praise and individuals never tried to grab the spotlight or beat their own chest.

One way we developed a culture of mutual support was having a time of recognition in staff meetings: a simple act that was low cost and high impact. We would take a moment to highlight team members who had performed especially well in a certain strategic area. For example, if we wanted to improve our contract accuracy, we would find someone who was doing a good job and bring positive attention to his performance in front of a group of peers.

We would offer verbal praise and also a small token of appreciation that he could associate with his good performance. A certificate, an award, or a special book would allow the team member to display his achievement and create opportunities for him to explain why he had received this gift. This ritual did more than give him recognition and reinforce his behavior; it created a lasting role model in the company.

You can get a lot more out of people with encouragement than with criticism. Even from the first days of Planet Tan, we used monthly meetings to recognize our top performers. We could see that what got measured got accomplished. If you add encouragement to that equation, people will break through walls and scale new heights for you. We knew that with the proper encouragement and support, our team members would accomplish more than they ever thought possible.

Not only did we encourage our team members, but, as mentioned earlier, we also sent letters of appreciation to their spouses or parents. This was another low-cost, high-reward investment. It's wonderful to receive a letter speaking highly about someone you love. From my own early career experiences, I could be fueled for weeks on one true word of praise from my superiors. Nothing else motivates like sincere admiration and appreciation.

American steel magnate Charles M. Schwab may have summed

it up best: "I consider my ability to rouse enthusiasm among the men the greatest asset I possess, and the way to develop the best that is in a man is by appreciation and encouragement. There is nothing else that so kills the ambitions of a man as criticisms from his superiors. I never criticize anyone. I believe in giving a man incentive to work. So I am anxious to praise and loathe to find fault. If I like anything, I am hearty in my approbation and lavish in my praise."

OFFERING GENUINE ENCOURAGEMENT

Although it's no secret that people like to be complimented on their hard work, going about it in a genuine way can be tricky. Saying "Thanks" is always appreciated, but there are other ways to provide real encouragement as well.

One underutilized method is to encourage by asking questions. Getting the other person talking about what's important to them and then actively listening to the response is a great way to encourage someone.

You can also encourage by reciprocation. This is used most effectively when the favor isn't returned in a reflex fashion. Instead of focusing on paying the other person back quickly, look for a special opportunity to do something nice for them that they wouldn't expect. The thought behind your actions is a powerful encourager that shows you care.

Tip 60

ASSOCIATE WITH WINNERS

Eagles don't fly with turkeys.
—Zig Ziglar

When Planet Tan first began, we were much smaller than the competition, but we had a big vision. One of the things we did from the get-go was to make a conscious and strategic decision to associate with things that would give us credibility and help make us a premier destination. We understood that if we could align Planet Tan with certain influencers and strategic partners, we could establish our brand more quickly and we could make ourselves seem much larger than we were.

During our first few years in business, Planet Tan was really in a "David and Goliath" competitive situation. We needed to make ourselves appear bigger, and we needed to give the customer a compelling reason to drive farther than the typical five to eight miles to try us out. In some cases, new customers would have to drive twenty-five miles to our location. The only way we could get people to go the extra miles was to make Planet Tan something special and compelling. We decided we could do this by associating ourselves with other organizations that were compelling.

I looked for opportunities to partner up with brands that matched our culture, our values, and our way of doing business. We looked for brands that were engaging and stylish; we wanted to associate ourselves with partners who were highly visible, but also relevant to our demographic. The first high-profile company we partnered with was the Dallas Stars NHL hockey franchise.

We created an unprecedented strategic alliance with the Dallas Stars in which their cheerleaders would be sponsored by Planet Tan. Once we started working with the Dallas Stars, you could say that the "stars" aligned, because, as I said earlier, not long after we began working with them in 1999, the Stars won the Stanley Cup! Eventually, our branding partnership evolved, and by 2007 the team's cheerleaders became known as the Planet Tan Ice Girls.

During the Stanley Cup series finals, in keeping with our irreverent, fun branding strategy, we handed out 18,000 white towels that bore Planet Tan's logo along with the slogan, "Tanned Fat Looks Better than Pale Fat." It was truly amazing to witness 18,000 screaming fans waving our Planet Tan towels at the Stanley Cup Championship series! At that point, Planet Tan became the "little company that could!" Later on we connected with the team's superstar Mike Modano, who became a spokesperson for Planet Tan. Again, it was all part of our strategy to align Planet Tan with trendsetters and influencers.

Once we had a successful partnership with the Dallas Stars, we set our sights on the other national sports franchises in Dallas. If working with the Stars was a coup, then getting the Mavs and the Cowboys would be a miracle, we decided. And getting billionaire entrepreneur and Dallas Mavericks owner Mark Cuban on board with Planet Tan would be the icing on the branding cake!

Fast-forward a bit, to the day when I was introduced to Mark Cuban at a Mavs game. We start talking about working together, and several e-mails later, he was on board with Planet Tan! Having Mark and the Mavericks associated with Planet Tan was huge; the impact of this partnership cannot be overstated. Even better, Mark became an advocate and a true supporter of Planet Tan. He was incredibly giving and helpful, and he really got involved. In fact, Mark was so closely associated with Planet Tan that people began thinking he was part owner. We had him in our print and radio ads, on our website, in point-of-purchase displays, in our recruitment video . . . we plastered him everywhere we could.

The partnership worked so well because Mark Cuban's personal brand—brash, cool, funny, and in-your-face—was perfectly aligned with the brand we were developing at Planet Tan. It was a match made in branding heaven! Mark was supportive and generous with his time and was very willing to push the envelope when it came to marketing and promotion. Needless to say, partnering with Mark Cuban and the Dallas Mavericks really enhanced Planet Tan's credibility and visibility. It's one of the keys that really made us look like a national brand.

The final piece of the associate-with-winners strategy came together when our chief competitor released their Dallas Cowboys sponsorship; we immediately swooped in and scooped it up. I looked at ways to maximize this new partnership and make it a big win for both organizations, and I got more involved in the marketing of the sponsorship. Planet Tan became the sponsor of the Dallas Cowboys Cheerleaders and their official tanning center.

One of the incredible benefits of being associated with the Dallas Cowboys Cheerleaders was that we became involved in their national Country Music Television reality television series, *Dallas Cowboys Cheerleaders: Making the Team*. This gave us national TV exposure and tremendous publicity. I even became a judge on the TV show during the Cowboys audition process. Since it was Planet Tan's job to help America's Sweethearts maintain their great appearance, we convinced CMT to include the Cheerleaders' tanning routine in the TV show. As CMT followed the Cheerleaders, they included shots of Planet Tan, along with shots of the girls tanning. This was "product placement" at its best, and represented hundreds of thousands of dollars' worth of free national television advertising!

Planet Tan's association with the Dallas sports franchises represented a "slam dunk" from a brand standpoint. Between being the first company to brand professional cheerleaders, to having Mark Cuban in our corner, to the national television exposure on CMT, we were really kicking on all cylinders. By creating strategic alliances with other influential, high-profile brands, we were able to skyrocket Planet Tan's visibility and appear "larger than life."

Now, your business may or may not be located in a market that makes associating with national sports franchises a possibility. However, you can still look for the winners in your area: people and organizations that are widely and quickly perceived as influential, positive, and admired. Identify these entities, and study ways that your product or service could be a fit with them. It's important to be sure that your overall image, message, and culture aligns with theirs in the broad themes; otherwise, you'll be presenting a conflicting branding message to your target market. The point is, time, effort, and money expended in creating this sort of strategic alliance will repay you a hundredfold in public acceptance, top-of-mind recognition, and, of course, sales.

Tip 61

FOLLOW MASTERFUL MENTORS

I bid him look into the lives of men as though into a
mirror, and from others to take an example for himself.
— *Terence*

It's not enough to surround yourself with winners; you've also got to have successful examples and mentors to follow. I shudder to think of where I'd be today if not for the support and counsel of wonderful mentors.

When I was younger, I relied on the advice of virtual mentors for guidance. My virtual board of advisers included historic figures such as Benjamin Franklin, self-help and motivational gurus like Napoleon Hill, and more modern corporate titans such as General Electric's Jack Welch. Fortunately, I've always been a voracious reader, and I devoured books by various thought leaders.

As I got older and more established in business, I met colleagues and friends who became trusted advisers. As a member of the Entrepreneurs' Organization (EO), I participate in meetings, conferences, and forums with other high-profile business owners and CEOs. Associations like these are invaluable and provide access to high-level players from all over the world.

There's an old piece of wisdom that says if you want to know how to get somewhere, ask someone you meet who's coming back from there. High-level networking groups like EO and MIT's "Birthing of Giants" program offer unique opportunities to meet and collaborate with other successful CEOs and business leaders.

In fact, I've been part of a "mastermind" EO group for more than eight years. We meet every month to brainstorm, share challenges and opportunities, and support each other. I consider these colleagues my personal board of directors, and their perspective and advice is priceless. They don't have a personal or financial stake in my company, so they can be objective. Plus, they've got years of experience in a number of different types of industries, so their point of view is extremely valuable.

In addition, since I've been with the same group over an extended period of time, we've developed a rhythm and a sixth sense about supporting each other. After all, we've had twelve meetings a year for eight years running—that's ninety-six meetings—with most of the original members of the group. A few have moved on for various reasons, and we've added others. But the core group has been together in excess of six years, which makes for a very powerful relationship; we've been able to develop a strong support system and friendships. We'll interview C-level job candidates for each other and help each other out whenever we can.

The forum has been one of the best business support groups I've ever been involved with, because not only did it help me grow and learn, but it also exposed me to new people and new ideas. A few of my forum colleagues in particular really encouraged me and motivated me to grow Planet Tan more quickly. I probably would not have been able to grow the company as aggressively if not for their input and encouragement. These guys are the ones who really pushed me to expand in the last few years. They all said, "You've got a great concept, but you've got to grow more quickly." So, in the final year that I owned the company, we built six new locations and expanded rapidly. That growth was a direct result of associating with guys who had big, successful companies and listening to advice from peers whom I respected that had smaller-sized companies. They knew that once I had the platform in place, I could scale it and grow faster. That kind of advice and motivation can only come from people you respect who've been there before.

The great thing about professional programs like EO and MIT's Birthing of Giants is that they expose you to some amazing entrepreneurs, and being surrounded by these folks really forces you to think bigger. Most of the people involved in EO or Birthing of Giants were running much bigger companies than I was, so it was a real inspiration to me. Before, I was like a little goldfish in a one-gallon tank, but after associating with all these other players, I realized that I could get big enough for a ten-gallon tank, a thirty-gallon tank—maybe my own pond! I realized, after being exposed to all of these different business leaders at different stages of success, that I needed to think more aggressively and move faster.

Listening to these business warriors was exciting for me; they convinced me that there was a whole other level of success out there, and my goal was to help get my company there. As a result, my confidence increased and my vision expanded. Once you see other people succeed, people who have a history of success and who are willing to share their knowledge and resources with you, you will discover and believe that you can do it, too.

Tip 62

REACH OUT AND REACH UP

The mediocre teacher tells. The good teacher explains.
The superior teacher demonstrates.
The great teacher inspires.
— William A. Ward

If you want to take your networking and your relationships with mentors to the next level, you've got to reach out and reach up. In other words, never be afraid to pick up the phone and call someone—no matter how high-and-mighty they may appear. It takes initiative, courage, and sometimes even a bit of audacity, but you should never shy away from meeting or talking with someone you can learn from.

I had read and followed former General Electric CEO Jack Welch for years, so when the opportunity arose to see him live and speak with him, I jumped at the chance. I attended a conference in Boston where the legendary GE leader was speaking, and I made damned sure I took advantage of the chance to introduce myself and talk with him in person. Meeting Jack Welch was the realization of yet another personal goal.

On another occasion, I had just finished reading a book about Nike, and I was so pumped up about it that I looked up Rob Strasser, the VP at Nike who was the real marketing mastermind behind the Nike brand. Rob had sold his Nike stock and purchased a microbrewery in Oregon. I contacted the microbrewery to see if I could reach Rob, but I was saddened to learn that he had passed away.

As it turned out, the gentleman I was speaking with about Rob was Bob Woodell, who had been Nike's first COO and who also went into the microbrewery business with Rob after leaving Nike. Just by picking up the phone and trying to reach someone, I ended up talking with Nike's second in command. You'd be surprised at how many people will talk to you and give you their time if you just make the effort to get on the phone and call these bigwigs!

I've never hesitated to reach out to seemingly inaccessible people if I thought I could learn something new from them. I've called well-known authors directly, and have contacted well-known CEOs and thought leaders from all over the world. Once I even contacted an author on Christmas Eve to ask him about his book, which I had just finished reading. Needless to say, I had expected to leave a message and wish him well during the holidays. I never thought I'd get to the author directly on Christmas Eve, but lo and behold, the author himself picked up the phone and was incredibly gracious. Perhaps even more surprising, we ended up having a great conversation for nearly an hour. Sometimes, famous people are much more accessible, approachable, and affable than you could ever imagine. Don't ever be afraid to reach out to them.

Tip 63

BEFRIEND YOUR COMPETITION

Leadership is based on inspiration, not domination;
on cooperation, not intimidation.
— *William Arthur Wood*

This may seem counterintuitive, but I always tried to embrace Planet Tan's competition and even befriend them. Don't get me wrong; we were very competitive and we played to win, but I always strove to maintain a good relationship with my direct competitors.

We wanted to be the best, so we'd share best practices and ideas with people from other industries, and even with people from within our own industry. Our greatest competition was not the tanning salon down the road, but ourselves: beating our own benchmarks and exceeding our own numbers. We looked at industry averages and studied who was best in class and then set out to blow those numbers away.

First, we'd compare how Planet Tan fared compared to industry averages, and then we'd look at the best in the business. What were they doing that we could do even better? How could we improve on their numbers? How could we come up with innovative ways to make our business better?

By the time we hit our stride, we were beating the competition as well as performing significantly above the average salon—and even beyond anyone in the industry. In fact, we had the highest sales per capita in the entire tanning business. We challenged ourselves to constantly exceed the competition's numbers. First we asked, "How can we double their numbers?" Then, once we hit that goal, we'd say, "How can we hit a million dollars in sales at one location?" We'd consistently benchmark our performance and get real-time feedback to stay on track.

All this time, I was never afraid to share ideas and information with the competition, as long as it was reciprocal. I've already related how, though my team members would get frustrated when they found out competitors were posing as customers in order to scope us out, I was never concerned by this. Instead, I believed we could learn from each other and make the entire industry better. After all, most of our success "secrets" were things any competitor could learn. They knew we were open 7 AM to 11 PM, seven days a week. They knew we had thirty to fifty tanning beds per location. They knew the kinds of numbers we were doing. We talked often and maintained an open relationship.

In fact, in the last year or so that I owned Planet Tan, I spoke with Rick Kueber, CEO of Suntan City, several times a week. While Suntan City didn't have locations in our backyard, they were a much larger chain than Planet Tan, with more than seventy stores. Still, there was a lot we could learn from each other, and we talked and traded information often. We studied how each other's company was doing things so we could both improve.

There was so much cooperation among our companies that anyone on my staff could call anyone on their staff anytime, and each staff would gladly assist the other. I wanted to know from Rick how he was growing his business, because they were so much larger than us in terms of locations; at the same time, Rick would pick my brain on how I was able to generate the level of revenue on a per-store basis, doing a million dollars per location. It was a relationship based on mutual trust and mutual benefit. That's the kind of openness and sharing I think you need if you really want to learn and grow. It also goes along with the idea of leaving your ego at the door; never allow yourself to believe you've got a corner on the market for good ideas.

I never really worried about sharing ideas with the competition, as long as we could learn from each other. After all, if you take the best team in the NFL and give their playbook to the worst team in the NFL, the losing team isn't suddenly going to become the number one team in the league. There are too many other factors at play: talent, discipline, execution, etc. It's not the ideas—it's the implementation of the ideas.

I always felt that there was something I could learn from everyone—competitor or not. For example, just one simple idea from Suntan City's Rick Kueber saved my company thousands of dollars. I learned from Rick that they were using DSL lines for their Internet, while we were using much more expensive fractional T1 lines. Rick's IT people explained to us that there was no competitive advantage to using the more expensive lines. Once we switched to DSL, we went from paying $500 per month to $70 per month. This meant we went from $6,000 in Internet access expense per year, per location, to $840 per location! That's a savings of more than $50,000 per year, just from that one tip.

I was generous in sharing my knowledge and ideas because I knew I'd receive knowledge and ideas in return. So, when my competitors asked me how we were able to pull in such large numbers, I'd tell them, "We've got long hours to make it convenient for our members; we have fifty beds so people don't have to wait; we've got three computers in the lobby for quick check-ins; we're extremely selective about the people we hire; and we do a really thorough job of training those people." They'd always ask, "But what else?" and I'd say: "That's it! That's what we do!" I think they were always looking for some silver bullet or magic idea, but our success was due to one thing: a consistently developed plan that was executed well, day in and day out. The key, of course, was being completely diligent in a few meaningful areas that had the highest impact in business.

In summary: Find out who the best person is in your industry, reach out to that person to find out what they're doing—what are their few critical areas of focus—and, if you're lucky, they'll share the information. Besides, maybe you have something to offer them in the knowledge exchange. There are also many business people who, if you are not in direct competition, would be glad to exchange ideas of mutual benefit. The key to this, of course, is to be as willing to give as you are to receive.

Tip 64

FIND YOUR "ANGEL"

The best teacher is the one who suggests rather than
dogmatizes, and inspires his listener with the wish
to teach himself.
— *Edward Bulwer-Lytton*

In addition to associating with winners and finding great mentors, consider yourself even more fortunate if you've found your "angel." My angel first appeared at the perfect time, when things were becoming increasingly tense with my business partner. He had invested when I first founded Planet Tan, and six years into the business, we were at odds on plans for growth and expansion.

Disagreements like this underscore the need for good shareholder documents and the importance of having solid buy-sell agreements. Unfortunately, I made the mistake of not creating some of these legal documents in the beginning, and I was paying for it when it came time to part ways.

In any event, it had become painfully apparent that my original partner and I had major philosophical differences about the future of Planet Tan; the time had come to buy out my partner. Again, I had excellent advisers and trusted colleagues whose counsel erased any doubts that I still had. One of the best tips I received was from Joe Croce, founder of the popular and successful Cici's Pizza, with over 650 locations in thirty states. He reminded me that it would never get any cheaper to buy him out than it was at that time. Joe hit the nail on the head. With the big plans I had for Planet Tan, it would only get more difficult and more expensive.

So I met my partner's price, and his original investment of $40,000 suddenly turned into a windfall of just south of $2 million. My partner would immediately become a wealthy man, but I'd have control of Planet Tan. Of course, I didn't have anywhere near that kind of money for the buyout. Until my "angel" appeared . . .

A year or so earlier, I had met Herb Sweetland, a very successful businessman from Tennessee, through a mutual friend. He was a serial entrepreneur, perhaps thirty or so years my senior. His wife owned a tanning business in Tennessee, and I went out there to help them out a bit. They were a wonderful couple, and I developed immense respect and admiration for them. Herb was the most unpretentious and down-to-earth entrepreneur I had ever met. He became a friend and a mentor, but he was about to become my angel.

I had a discussion with Herb, and he agreed to invest in the company for a stake in Planet Tan. Using that infusion of cash, plus financing with an attractive interest rate, I was able to make my partner an offer he couldn't refuse. Meanwhile, thanks to my angel investor, I'd now gone from 50 percent ownership of the company to 80 percent ownership. All I had to do was take on more debt, but it gave me majority ownership and it extracted me from the onerous partnership. Everyone came out a winner.

You could say my angel reappeared again not long afterward. Now I owned 80 percent of Planet Tan, but Herb was insightful (and generous) enough to know that, ultimately, I wanted to be the sole owner of my company.

Herb magnanimously offered to sell me the remaining 20 percent of the company for only a reasonable amount more than he had invested, and he even helped me finance the transaction. So once again, with creative financing that didn't force me to raise an enormous amount of cash, I was able to buy my partner's stake in the company. I was now the sole, 100-percent owner of Planet Tan; my longtime dream was finally realized. As I've mentioned earlier, this wouldn't have happened without gaining insights from experienced businesspeople, associating with successful people, joining groups that helped me meet potential investors, and having top-notch accounting and financial metrics.

In fact, if you find yourself in a situation similar to mine, remember that many accounting firms have clients who are looking for investment opportunities and may be able to get the two of you together. The key is to get out there and meet people who can help you learn and grow. Also, never fail to make yourself available to assist others in business. You can never be sure where these relationships lead, and one of them may end up identifying your angel.

Tip 65

CREATE PRIDE IN THE ORGANIZATION

Show class, have pride, and display character.
If you do, winning takes care of itself.
— Coach Paul "Bear" Bryant

Finding the right people, celebrating successes, and taking good care of the team all cultivate a positive company culture that inspires enthusiasm and motivation. At Planet Tan, we had a mission, we had confidence, and we were fired up. This atmosphere created pride in the organization and a belief that we could accomplish anything. "Make history" was more than a slogan; it was our mission.

In the early days of Planet Tan, we established rituals, which we called traditions. Every month we went to a hotel meeting space or a restaurant and celebrated the top salespeople. We kept the team motivated and pumped up. We were building our brand on sheer motivation, inspiration, and good old-fashioned hard work. Back then, I was probably more like a cheerleader than a CEO. But it was important that we develop that pride in the company, and creating traditions was the first step.

One could argue that creating pride in our organization was especially challenging because, as I've mentioned, we were in an industry that typically didn't have a great reputation. At the time, tanning was more of a mom-and-pop, back room business, almost on the seedy side; we had to legitimize the entire industry and create a positive atmosphere in the workplace at the same time. Fortunately, we brought in our genuine values and a very strong work ethic.

Although our values might have been old-fashioned, the brand we were building was anything but. From day one, we developed Planet Tan as an appealing, trendy, and sassy brand; it was all about youth, energy, and a positive environment. I suppose you could say that we took tanning out of the back room and into the limelight. We created a place where team members could thrive and guests could have a great experience every time they visited our stores.

I've already mentioned our "Traditions" class that we developed for new team members. In the class, we would discuss who we were, what we were all about, and how the new people could grow and succeed within the company. This was just one of the ways we created pride in the organization. I've also talked about our Bronze Book, a small booklet that our staff could keep with them to reinforce our beliefs and culture. The Bronze Book was more of a guide to our mission than an employee handbook, but it helped to reinforce the forward-thinking, positive culture we were cultivating. We were building an organization that everyone could be excited about and proud of.

Key Insights on Staying Positive

- Do you set BHAGs for your company? Why is it important to think big? How do you keep your goals visible and at the forefront of your business? Is your team held accountable for meeting short- and long-term company goals? What are six key themes for growth?

- How do you provide real encouragement to your employees? What tactics do you employ to show appreciation and reinforce positive behavior? Are they effective?

- With whom does your company associate? Do you have a tendency to seek out winners? Brainstorm local and national brands that you admire. How can you become partners with them? Don't be afraid to reach up and out.

- In addition to associating with winners, you need to have strong personal and virtual mentors. Do you have a network of business leaders with whom you meet regularly? If not, how could you go about forming such a group?

- Who is your competition? Do you have a good relationship with them? How might you cultivate a positive working relationship that is mutually beneficial?

CHAPTER 8

PROMISE

Promises are an important communication tool that build trust and express responsibility and reliability. Many companies offer a satisfaction guarantee to assure the customer of an acceptable transaction. But the customers aren't the only ones who need to feel secure in dealing with your business. You make a promise to the customer to go the extra mile, but you also make a promise to your employees to reward excellence with the proper incentives. This chapter will show you how to make and deliver on promises to customers, employees, and yourself.

Tip 66

CONCENTRATE YOUR EFFORTS

Concentration is my motto — first honesty,
then industry, then concentration.
— Andrew Carnegie

In business, you can't be all things to all people, nor can you compete on every front. Not everything can or should be important. You've got to focus on your core competencies and concentrate your efforts. What is your primary area of focus? What is the narrow niche that you will carve out for yourself? You simply can't be the best at everything.

One of the books and philosophies we adopted at Planet Tan was called *The Myth of Excellence: Why Great Companies Never Try to Be the Best at Everything*, by Fred Crawford and Ryan Matthews. The authors explain that there are essentially five key areas in which a company can compete: access, experience, price, product, and service. Crawford and Matthews suggest that successful businesses are those who excel in one of these areas, are good in another, and are at least average in the rest. For example, Wal-Mart competes first and foremost on price, whereas Nordstrom focuses primarily on service. The authors conclude that it is impossible to be excellent in all areas. It's also impractical to attempt to market your business based on more than one or two key attributes.

In order to differentiate your company from the competition and effectively build your brand, you need to focus on your core strength and find that one area where you can truly excel. For Planet Tan, our primary focus was access, while our secondary attribute was experience. The way we differentiated ourselves from everyone else was by providing unprecedented and unmatched access.

1. Access

The Planet Tan brand was built on access. To us, access meant cleanliness, no waiting for a tanning bed, and more convenient hours. We had more tanning beds so our members never had to wait. We had three computers at the front desk instead of one, so members could check in quickly and easily. We had five phone lines so callers never got a busy signal. We were open 7:00 AM until 11:00 PM, seven days a week, which gave our members much greater access to the facilities than the competition offered. We hired bed cleaners, whose job was to keep our tanning rooms immaculate. All of these innovations and conveniences were designed to reinforce our focus on access.

2. Experience

Access was our primary differentiator, and experience was our secondary driver. Experience was the overall member experience from the moment the member arrives in our parking lot to the moment they leave. Experience is the look and feel and tone of our stores; the way the member is treated by our team; the architecture; the music in the tanning rooms—all the little details that add up to a remarkable experience for our members.

I've already discussed our goal of providing a "10" member experience. We were able to use it to differentiate ourselves, because everything about Planet Tan took the member experience into consideration. It was everything from our design and architecture to our attitude. Once we started advertising, our marketing was also very cool and edgy. More important, the experience delivered on the brand promise. When members or guests walked into one of our stores, there was never a disconnect with the expectations our marketing put in place. The experience was consistent and was played out in every detail at Planet Tan. None of this would have been possible without concentrating our efforts and staying laser focused on only the primary and secondary attributes of our brand: access and experience.

Look at your business. What are you really good at; why do your customers love your business? If you're just starting out, how are you going to be different and make yourself matter to potential customers? Choose how you are going to define yourself, and then work like mad to be the very best at your point of difference, making sure you're not trying to put equal energy into everything at once. Choose the most important point of differentiation for your business, and feed all your energy into making it happen.

Tip 67

THE BRAND IS IN THE DETAILS

*The great successful men of the world have used their
imaginations, they think ahead and create their mental picture,
and then go to work materializing that picture in all its
details, filling in here, adding a little there, altering this a bit
and that a bit, but steadily building, steadily building.*
— *Robert Collier*

A brand is built on details; a thousand little things can add up over time to create your brand. As I mentioned earlier, at Planet Tan we called this the sixth sense: the experience that the member gets — an almost unconscious, but powerful, feeling built on an accumulation of the smallest details. Although our members couldn't necessarily point to one thing that made the Planet Tan experience memorable, they knew that they felt better when they left than when they came.

I've already talked about how we believed at Planet Tan that "everything matters." Since our business and our brand were both based on access and experience, we were fanatical about every last detail that went into the member experience, since we knew that the cumulative effect would be the way our brand was defined by our public. We were relentless in our pursuit of the perfect member experience, and we reviewed and studied every touch point that we had with our members. Many of these touch points or details may have seemed small or inconsequential, but all the little things added up to the unique experience that defined our brand.

We combined strategy, technology, and process to ensure that the member experience was extraordinary on every visit to Planet Tan. Nothing was left to chance, and every last aspect of the member's visit was taken into consideration. From the design and architecture of our stores to the hooks and hangers in the tanning rooms, the entire atmosphere was intentional.

For example, we replaced single doors with double doors at our entrances, so that there would never be a jam at the front door. We studied ergonomics and traffic patterns so that we knew to move member card scanners closer to the door. We even did "time stamp studies" to determine how to make the member check-in more efficient and convenient. We reduced our first-time customer check-in process from one minute to thirty-eight seconds by studying and improving the transaction time.

Because 78 percent of our clients were female, safety was a concern—so we made sure that our lobbies and parking lots were brightly lit and welcoming. To give our members an even greater sense of safety and security, our tanning rooms had big, industrial, 42-inch-wide doors with solid, stainless-steel hardware. A heavy, secure door with high-quality locks and handles helped our female members feel safe and comfortable in our tanning rooms.

Cleanliness was another important element that went into the "10" member experience, so we were zealous about keeping our stores and our tanning rooms immaculate. Every member who visited Planet Tan and entered the tanning room was made to feel like she was the first person ever to set foot in the room. The equipment sparkled, and a plush Planet Tan towel was folded and waiting. Just like at a five-star hotel, guests would feel like the room was brand-new, simply waiting for their arrival. Of course, fresh towels for every member means you've got to constantly have a full supply on hand so you never run out, so some stores had 500 towels on hand—meaning even things like storage had to be considered.

The experience was further enhanced by the atmosphere in the stores, including not only the design but also the signage, graphics, and even the music in the tanning rooms. Our signs were big and bold, so all the necessary member information was easy to find and easy to understand. We had big signboards with membership details and pricing, so a new visitor to Planet Tan could see the information for themselves if they weren't ready to personally engage one of our team members. It's a bit like listing the menu outside a restaurant, so potential guests don't feel intimidated while they check things out.

As for the music, we had our own custom mix of music in the lobby to embellish the atmosphere and add to the cool vibe. Here we borrowed an idea from Starbucks and made sure that the mix was uniquely crafted to fit our brand. Once members entered the tanning rooms, they had their choice of six different musical genres to listen to while they tanned. We researched musical tastes by location and programmed the music based on the results of our surveys. We even took the innovative step, in partnership with our equipment vendor, of introducing the first tanning beds with the music source built directly into the bed!

All of these details were designed to exceed members' expectations and build our brand based on access and experience. In order to create a perception of a brand that was rock solid and reliable in our members' minds, we had to deliver on our promise and we had to do it consistently. Members had to be offered the same level of extraordinary service, whether it was 7:00 AM on a Wednesday morning or 10:30 PM on a Sunday night.

Tip 68

EXCEED EXPECTATIONS

Always render more and better service than what is
expected of you, no matter what your task may be.
— *Og Mandino*

As you can tell from our uncompromising attention to detail, the Planet Tan brand was built on consistently exceeding expectations. Obviously, the member experience we created was designed to exceed expectations at every touch point, but the real difference was our people. I've already said it but it's so important that it bears repeating: We had the same equipment as the tanning salon down the road—the thing that made Planet Tan truly distinctive was the experience created by our team.

The truth is that we could have automated the entire process with swipe cards, bar codes, and technology. In fact, some tanning salons in Europe do just that. In effect, those tanning salons become self-serve facilities—high-tech, low-touch. But our unique selling proposition was the polar opposite. Not only did we have the human interaction, but our team members also developed a real relationship with our members and created an emotional connection that enhanced the member experience.

We were able to consistently exceed expectations because we provided a relationship and an experience, not just a transaction. Our team really cared about our members and showed genuine interest in them. We created a culture at Planet Tan that was designed to support our members and build rapport with them. We made sure that we knew our members personally and that we took an interest in their lives. We went out of our way to make sure that our members knew how much we appreciated them. Because we took the time and effort to build real relationships with our members, it became impossible for competitors to replicate the Planet Tan experience. Our experience couldn't be commoditized or replaced by a "bargain-price" strategy, because we offered something much more than a transaction based on price.

Our team members showed concern and compassion for our members, whether it was with a sincere compliment, going out of their way to help the member, or just giving great tanning advice. We'd make every effort to do all the little things for our members that would add up to an extraordinary experience. Our mission was to make people feel better about themselves, and that included not just the tanning itself, but the entire member experience at Planet Tan.

We worked hard to make sure that we stayed relevant to our members, so all the little extras and attention to detail we provided combined to create an amazing experience. What we were really doing was building the business one member at a time.

Fortunately, we created a culture where it mattered to us to do good work and to genuinely care about our members. In fact, we'd always look for "hero" stories or examples that demonstrated how our team went above and beyond to serve our members and deliver an extraordinary experience, and then we made these victory stories a part of our corporate culture. We'd often start our staff meetings or conference calls by asking for any recent hero stories. When we found an example of a team member doing something amazing for our members, we shared that story throughout the company. We'd recognize and reward this behavior because we knew that what gets reinforced gets repeated.

I recall a particular example of going above and beyond for our members. An anxious bride-to-be wanted to be tanned for her wedding day, but she got so busy the day before her wedding that she never made it in to Planet Tan. She finally showed up with her bridesmaids at 11:00 PM—precisely the time we closed. However, the Planet Tan team member on duty kept the store open for her so she and her bridesmaids could use Versa Spa Sunless Booth, a spray-on tan that makes you look like you just walked off the beach. Our employee had to stay until midnight, but she made sure that the bride got everything she needed and that she looked terrific for her big day. A few days later, the employee that had kept the store open for the bride received a nice thank-you card and a photo from the wedding. Everyone lived happily ever after, and we had yet another hero story that served as an example of creating the "10" member experience.

Any business or service professional can look for ways to go the extra mile and stay relevant to customers. It doesn't matter whether you're a plumber, a piano teacher, or a lawyer; you can avoid being "commoditized" if you're willing to exceed expectations and deliver exceptional service. This can take the form of a simple act or a small detail that makes the difference and sets you apart. For the plumber, it might mean making a special house call to help out a customer on Christmas Eve. For the piano teacher, perhaps it's surprising your student with free concert tickets or tracking down a hard-to-find CD for her. The point is that you can create a culture of caring in your company as long as you are committed to delivering an extraordinary experience for your clients each and every day.

Tip 69

GO FOR "SHARE OF HEART"

Win hearts, and you have all men's hands and purses.
— William Cecil Burleigh

Having your customer's "share of mind" is good; having a "share of heart" is even better. Share of heart means that your clients are emotionally invested in your company. Not only are they fans of your brand, but they are also evangelists for your business. There's nothing better than a customer who is passionate about you, because he will help your company grow and flourish. Those passionate customers will create buzz and word of mouth about your company, whether through referrals or by using social media—and in this day and age, you can never forget the impact of resources like Facebook, Twitter, MySpace, and other similar outlets.

So, while it's important to earn your customers' share of mind, you should also work tirelessly to capture their share of heart. We were able to earn share of heart with our members because our culture, our brand, and our team created an emotional bond with them. We connected with our members, and we were excited that the member had decided to spend some time with us. This authentic sense of caring helped solidify the relationship and build our share of heart with our members.

Any business can easily find out who its top customers are: amount of spending, time with the company, number of referrals, growth in account, and other factors. Something as small as a handwritten letter to them, letting your very best customers know how important they are to the success of the company, can make a world of difference in differentiating you from your competition and giving these customers an incentive to become "raving fans." Never lose an opportunity to acknowledge their loyalty and show your appreciation. Create special clubs that are exclusive to this group of loyal customers. Provide them with easy ways to pass the word out about your business; do things that allow them special access or privileges. And don't forget to use their names a lot! Showing appreciation for their choice of your product or service can help you win share of heart.

Tip 70

DESIGN THE BRAND AND BRAND THE DESIGN

Design is not just what it looks like and feels like.
Design is how it works.
— Steve Jobs

Planet Tan started out with three locations that we inherited from the previous ownership of the tanning salons. However, when it came time to expand and open our fourth location, we knew we had an opportunity to make a statement. The new location would be the first that we would build from the ground up, so it was the ideal time to create the overall look and feel of Planet Tan. I realized that design could be a competitive advantage, and that the architecture could play an important role in establishing and distinguishing our brand.

I turned to designs I admired. I've already mentioned how I loved the chic, modern look of Crunch Fitness and the New York Health & Racquet Club, so I tracked down the architect behind those companies, Frank Denner. Frank was known for clean, high-end design; his approach to architecture is anything but cookie-cutter, so I knew he'd be the perfect fit for Planet Tan.

Frank came to Dallas and we looked at competitors and other businesses to determine what we did *not* want. Other tanning salons were too generic, too vanilla. We wanted our members to feel relaxed and looking forward to spending time with us when they came in; we also wanted a totally new look for a tanning salon. Frank created a unique look and feel for Planet Tan that captured perfectly our youth and vitality, as well as our sense of fun and energy. The design was vibrant, fresh, and stylish.

I recently asked Frank about his inspiration for the design, and he says that much of what he wanted to do with the architecture of Planet Tan was to capture our energy and enthusiasm. He knows that I'm a very passionate guy, and he wanted the design to embody that passion in the store. The moment someone walked into a Planet Tan location, he said, they should feel like they are some place fun and special—a place where they can escape for a while and leave feeling much better than before they arrived. Frank nailed the design of Planet Tan, and the look and feel of our stores became another key differentiator and embodiment of the brand.

When customers come into contact with your business, what is the feeling that you want them to have? It's important that your design—your architecture, floor plan, and fixtures—create a positive, interesting, emotional response. You don't want them to feel that they've entered a bland box that feels like everything else out there.

Read design magazines; look at businesses that have a certain feel that you would like your business to emulate. Find out who did the work for the business and talk to the provider to determine if you can hire them to work with you.

It's also important to understand that great design does not have to cost lots of money. Be clear about who your customers are and what type of feeling you want them to have when doing business with your company. Then go out and get the best person to help you create that feeling. Your design is one of the most important things you can do to make a good first impression. Great design is a game changer.

Tip 71

EXPAND THE BRAND

Create the kind of climate in your organization where
personal growth is expected, recognized, and rewarded.
—*Author unknown*

After a few years, Planet Tan had built a solid brand identity. We were very conscious of all the little things that go into developing a brand, and we were careful to keep the brand consistent in all of our activities. Every detail, every contact with the customer, and everything about the experience combined to create our unique brand experience.

We realized that we needed a brand mascot, or an icon that would symbolize the Planet Tan brand, but we didn't want a particular person or a swimsuit model or a celebrity spokesperson. Instead, we needed something or someone who was more universal, more accessible, and more representative of our brand. To get the perfect representation, we decided, we had to create it. Thus, Betty was born.

Of course, we couldn't just whip up any cartoon character; Betty deserved better. So we went to Hollywood and commissioned a top cartoon illustrator so that we'd have an amazing, comic book–like character. After a few tries and some incredible artwork, we had a winner. Betty became the official mascot and virtual spokeswoman of Planet Tan.

Betty was perfect for Planet Tan; she could be fun without being silly, sexy without being too provocative, and stylish without being inaccessible. As a cartoon character, Betty could take on whatever brand attributes we assigned to her. Depending on the situation, Betty could be in a bikini or doing yoga. And just like Planet Tan, Betty was young, fun, savvy, stylish, and, of course, tan.

We incorporated our corporate mascot into our training program, urging our team members to "be Betty":

BE **B**EAUTIFUL

BE **E**NTHUSIASTIC

BE **B**RILLIANT

BE **E**MPOWERED

BE **T**AN

BE **T**ENACIOUS

BE **Y**OU

In addition to adopting our vivacious and colorful mascot, Planet Tan also began leveraging the brand through our own private line of tanning lotions. Obviously, we were interested in the ancillary revenues the products could provide, but we were much more motivated to develop our own branded lotions because it would give us further control over the member experience and would again differentiate Planet Tan from the competition.

Our custom tanning lotions were not some generic product with a Planet Tan label slapped on, either. These products had been carefully tested and developed to appeal to our members and their specific tanning needs. Like everything else about Planet Tan, our tanning lotions were unique and unlike anything else offered by the competition. From the ingredients, the packaging, and right down to the shipping boxes and the display, everything about the product had to reflect our brand. It was all part of the seamless communication of the Planet Tan brand.

Once the line of tanning lotions became more popular, we resisted the urge to make them available elsewhere. As the sentinels of the Planet Tan brand, we made a conscious decision that our lotions would only be available at our stores or on our website. We designed the product so that when using it, our members would deepen their emotional connection to Planet Tan; controlling the entire process was crucial.

Our first custom tanning product line was called EGO, obviously playing off our "Feed Your Ego" tagline. We purposely did not name the product itself after Planet Tan, although there was a small Planet Tan logo at the bottom of the bottle. The first product was called EGO Fire 3, and it was a tanning accelerator designed for the active tanner. This came in an orange bottle and had a "tingle" factor so that users knew it was hot. At $50 per bottle, it was a high-end product made for the serious tanner. Eventually, we rolled out five products in the EGO line, including EGO Hemp, a popular post-tan product made with hempseed oil to hydrate and moisturize the skin after tanning.

The next line in our family of tanning products was named after our mascot, Betty. The Betty line was more affordable, and featured three different lotions: Lovely Betty, Charming Betty, and Sexy Betty. Our Betty character became so popular that she not only had a line of tanning lotions named after her, but we also had Betty beach towels, Betty T-shirts, and even Betty beach balls. Originally, the beach balls were props for our stores, but our members went crazy for them—so we started giving them away.

Our third line of products came about as a result of customer feedback and the organic craze that was sweeping the nation. We created our Organix lotion as a healthy, natural lotion with no preservatives. It contained antiaging ingredients and antioxidants, and it featured a light eucalyptus fragrance. Later, we even offered Organix candles: natural, soy-based candles.

All of our products were carefully designed to expand the brand and enhance the overall member experience. Every detail was taken into consideration as we rolled out new products. With the lotions, we paid attention to the color, the ingredients, the packaging design, the scent, and even the viscosity of the lotion and how it felt going on the skin. All these factors had to be considered to ensure that the product supported and promoted the Planet Tan brand.

As you consider your business and your brand, look for ways to solve more of your customers' problems; these will be areas where you may be able to expand your services—as long as it does not distract you from your core business and improves or is complementary to your central business offering. Finding these needs and meeting them allows you to connect on more levels with your customer, offering a better opportunity for you to grow the relationship and your share of the customer's business.

TEACH A MAN TO FISH

Give a man a fish and you feed him for a day.
Teach a man to fish and you feed him for a lifetime.
— *Chinese proverb*

We lived the brand by associating with the major sports franchises, but this effort also extended to local charities and community organizations. We felt that giving back to the community was an important part of our corporate culture; we wanted this to become integral with who we were as a company.

Aside from our strategic partnerships with the major teams in Dallas, we supported a community charity called the Nexus Recovery Center, an organization that helped disadvantaged women get back on their feet. We decided early on that we wanted to share our success with the community, since the community was the source of our success.

As a young organization, we found that many of our team members wanted to be involved in giving back in the community, but they didn't know exactly how to get started or where to go. Nevertheless, the staff loved having a way to participate. In fact, I've found most people do want to help others out, and when they do, they feel good about themselves, as well. We found it to be a great morale booster for the staff to realize that there was much more to business than just earning for yourself. We also realized that this effort positioned our company not just as a group of tanning salons, but as a responsible business that wanted to share for the betterment of others.

I believe people more than ever are realizing that material things will not ultimately generate happiness, but that helping others is fulfilling, providing something that money cannot. If this belief applies to your company, I recommend getting your organization behind a worthy cause; it's a wonderful way to unite your people and a great way for them to see another dimension of your business.

Our philosophy for supporting charities harkened back to the familiar saying quoted at the beginning of this section, "Give a man a fish and he eats for a day; teach a man to fish and he eats for a lifetime." We had tremendous respect and admiration for the less fortunate people who were "learning to fish" and doing everything they could to get their lives together.

We connected with the Nexus Recovery Center because they support women battling substance abuse; single mothers who need help with their children while they're in recovery; and young women who are trying to put their lives back together. As the son of a single mother who faced adversity and persevered, I felt a deep connection with this organization. We also liked supporting Nexus because they helped the children of these mothers. Kids are often the innocent bystanders in these situations, and Nexus had facilities to care for the kids while their moms were in recovery.

The first year that we were involved with Nexus, we asked the organization to identify one mother who was a success story in the making so we could do more to help her get her life back together. The eventual candidate had two young kids, so at Christmas, we gave each of our stores a budget for our team members to buy Christmas presents for the kids.

Then, when we had our staff holiday party, we invited the mom and her kids and gave the young boys the Christmas gifts our team members had purchased. The kids were absolutely thrilled and our team members got to really connect with the family. Because we also wanted to do something special for the mom, our chief operating officer picked her up in a limousine and took her shopping to get new business clothes, and we also treated her to a makeover. To us, this was so much better and more fulfilling than simply writing a check to a charity.

After that first year, we started going to Nexus during the holidays to distribute Christmas gifts to all the kids. We also gave gifts to the staff at Nexus for their dedication and hard work. It was the beginning of a holiday tradition for Planet Tan that gave us the chance to make a difference in the community. We really identified with the women and children at Nexus, because these were women who were really trying to get their lives back on track and become self-sufficient. Working with Nexus also turned out to be an important life lesson for our young team members; truly a win-win.

Tip 73

BUILD A BETTER BRAND

A brand for a company is like a reputation for a person.
You earn reputation by trying to do hard things well.
—Jeff Bezos

I've always been a student of great advertising and marketing, so when it came time to really develop a brand for Planet Tan, I called in the best advertising executives in the country. I looked at the brands and the companies I admired, and went after the talent responsible for creating those brands. As I mentioned, Crunch Fitness founder Doug Levine put me in touch with Tom DelMundo, a top advertising executive at DDB in New York City. I got Tom on the phone and convinced him to take a look at what we were doing in Dallas.

Tom admits now that he thought the Planet Tan gig would be a quick, fun little project. Fifteen years later, we're great friends and still working together. Tom was instrumental in developing the marketing and advertising for Planet Tan and was, in many ways, the architect of the brand. Even though he was in New York and we had a virtual working relationship (we didn't meet face-to-face until four years after we began working together), Tom played a huge role in our success.

Tom helped us create our mascot, Betty, and he helped give our advertising a very professional, "national-brand" feel. Tom became our branding watchdog and made sure that everything we did was true to the brand—fun, youthful, hip, and irreverent.

However, a brand cannot grow and endure without being embraced by each and every employee, who in turn passes it on to each and every customer or client. Planet Tan did many things to instill the essence of the brand with our team members, from orientation and ongoing training to frequent meetings and company rituals.

In addition to living the brand each day, Tom also created a brand bible, which contained detailed information and guidelines pertaining to every aspect of the Planet Tan brand. These branding guidelines made it clear to our team members and our strategic partners exactly how the brand should be portrayed—whether in print, on the radio, in our stores, or at live events.

Our branding guidelines ensured that everyone had a very specific path to follow when working on ads or promotions or in-store activities. You'll see, from excerpts from The Brand Book below, that there was never any question about how we wanted to represent the Planet Tan brand.

EXCERPTS FROM PLANET TAN'S BRAND BOOK

Great brands are not born, they're built: one step at time. The goal of this document is to provide a clear and consistent guide to the Planet Tan brand essence, visual aesthetic, and standards of excellence.

About the Company:

Founded in 1995 in Dallas, Texas, Planet Tan has over fifteen locations in the Dallas-Metro area. Planet Tan is a pioneer in indoor tanning with a brand based on fun, honesty, and hipness with a sense of humor.

The Company Mission:

Work hard. Have fun. Make history.

The Brand Promise:

Planet Tan is more stylish and fun than any other tanning center and provides an unsurpassed tanning experience.

The Brand Personality:

Planet Tan is hip, flirty, clever, sassy, truthful, and above all, fun.

Brand Association:

Planet Tan positions itself with other fun and hip brands that challenge and dominate in their industries:

PLANET TAN vs. NOT PLANET TAN		
W-hotels	vs.	Hilton
SKYY vodka	vs.	Jack Daniels
Mini Cooper	vs.	Ferrari
Target	vs.	Wal-Mart
Ben & Jerry's	vs.	Häagen-Dazs
Paul Frank	vs.	Gap
Apple or Dell	vs.	Microsoft/etc.

The Logo and Tagline:

The brand mark consists of the "planet and ring" and the words "Planet Tan". . .

> The tagline "Feed your ego" encapsulates the brand in its honesty and humor . . .

The Color and Texture Palette:

Used consistently over time, colors become associated with companies: UPS brown and Coca-Cola red are a few examples . . .

Betty:

The official mascot of Planet Tan, she is the virtual spokeswoman and a key piece of brand equity. She personifies Planet Tan's core target market: young, hip, vivacious, and tan.

> Like Mickey Mouse for Disney or Erin for eSurance, Betty can change her costume to fit any occasion . . .

Advertising Tone and Manner:

Planet Tan's award-winning print, radio, and TV ads have been a hallmark of the brand since its inception. It's key that the ads remain on the cutting edge but remain relevant to the consumer, our business, and above all, true to the brand.

The ads have always had a sense of humor and wit . . .

We avoid the clichés of hot women in bikinis and low-brow sexuality, except when done in jest or irony . . .

Core Target Audience:

Women, age 28–35; single or young moms. Fitness conscious and upwardly mobile. Upper-middle-class incomes. Live or work within five miles of a Planet Tan location.

Summary:

Hopefully now you have a good grasp of what Planet Tan looks like, sounds like, and feels like. The work you create . . . should sell both the product as well as the essence of the brand . . . hip, flirty, clever, sassy, truthful, fun, and above all, a great tan . . .

Brand Comparison:

As a final litmus test, look at the work you have created and ask yourself, is it as cool as work created for these brands?

W-hotels
SKYY vodka
Mini Cooper
Target
Ben & Jerry's
Paul Frank
Apple

If you can honestly say yes, then it's probably good enough to be for Planet Tan.

In designing the marketing concept for your business, once you have your logo, font, design, and even your colors, it's time to start working on your guidelines. As you can see from the detailed plan shown above (and this is just an excerpt from the full, detailed document), having this important marketing document will help you stay on track. It will also aid other people who create marketing collateral for your business to stay within a scope that you have defined. The more clearly you know how and to whom you want to present yourself, the better your marketing will become.

Over time, if the marketing work is done well, people will begin to recognize your ads and separate them from the clutter they are being exposed to every day. That's why all your messages need to tie back to a clear brand design. Eventually you will start building your brand equity: the value being created from all of the advertising you've been spending money on.

Tip 74

RUN YOUR BUSINESS LIKE YOU'RE GOING TO RUN IT FOREVER

Drive thy business or it will drive thee.
— *Benjamin Franklin*

About eight years into running Planet Tan, I started to get inquiries about selling the company. While I wasn't personally or professionally ready to do that, the sale offers did force me to start thinking more about the value of the company and let me know that I did have options.

As intriguing and thought provoking as those initial offers were, some of the best business advice I ever received was to run my business as if I were going to run it forever. This is a very wise philosophy, because the minute you start thinking like a seller instead of an owner, you begin making decisions differently.

The decisions a seller or investor makes about a business differ greatly from decisions made by someone who has a long-term view, someone who plans to be running the business indefinitely.

Once you start thinking like a seller rather than an owner, you begin to look for ways to grow your margins or improve your bottom line — often at the expense of customer service. Maybe you don't invest in that new software or hire that new manager. You look for ways to cut and save, and that's obviously not in the best interest of growing the company. You try to squeeze extra value out of the business instead of taking the long view.

Here's something else to consider: If you're running your business with an eye toward selling, what happens if the sale falls through? Then you're not positioned to grow. All of a sudden, you've got a business that doesn't have that new location, that didn't invest in that new accounting software. You've abandoned your growth strategy in favor of a sale . . . that didn't happen. That's why the best advice is to run and manage your business as if you're going to be running it well into the future.

Fortunately, my business goals were in line with my personal goals, so I turned away offers to sell while there were still many opportunities to continue to grow, both personally and professionally.

Tip 75

KNOW WHEN TO EXIT THE STAGE

Success is a journey, not a destination.
— Arthur Ashe

How do you know when it's time to walk away from the business you've created? How can you be sure when the time has come to step aside and let your baby go on without you? It's as much a personal decision as it is a business decision. You've got to be ready not just financially and operationally, but psychologically as well. You must ask yourself: Have you accomplished all you set out to do, and can you exit the stage knowing you have achieved a level of mastery?

I've always believed that no success arrives fully formed; you've got to put in years of hard work to achieve any level of mastery. I agree with Malcolm Gladwell's 10,000-hour rule as presented in his 2008 bestseller *Outliers*. Gladwell pointed out that the key to success in any field is due in large measure to practicing a specific task for a total of 10,000 hours. A lot of what we describe as talent, argues Gladwell, is really just a willingness to work very, very hard for a long period of time. Certainly talent and aptitude play a role, but you've got to put in the time to master your craft.

Greatness requires an enormous amount of time and practice. Following Gladwell's 10,000-hour rule would require twenty hours of work a week for ten years. That sounds fairly accurate from my perspective; I was really beginning to have a firm grasp on my business by about year seven. And, while I can honestly say that the years of practice and apprenticeship were starting to pay off by the time Planet Tan was seven years old, it would be a few more years before I felt I had truly mastered the business. By the time I considered selling the company, I was totally knowledgeable about the business, having put in the hours, months, and years to achieve a high level of proficiency. I felt very empowered and confident about the business, and I had attained a tremendous level of satisfaction, believing that I'd done everything with Planet Tan that I set out to do.

After thirteen years, we had a scalable, sustainable, and successful business that could continue to grow without its founder. I had accomplished my personal and professional goals, and I was now in a position to consider selling Planet Tan.

Some of the benefits of receiving offers to sell the business include getting an estimated valuation of your company, along with realizing that you do have options and you can begin to at least consider an exit strategy. It's always helpful to get a sense of what the market thinks your business is worth. It gives you an outside opinion for a valuation for your company, which can also be tremendously helpful as you're dealing with banks or investors. It can be a bit of a reality check as well.

The first time I was approached with an offer to sell Planet Tan, there was a real offer on the table, so it validated that my business had developed to the point that a sale was possible. Still, I wasn't ready to sell, both because I loved what I did and because there was still a long way to go to get Planet Tan where I really wanted it to be as a business. It was too early in the life cycle of the company and in my personal path as an entrepreneur. I had a bigger vision for Planet Tan, and I still needed time to put strategies in place to make the company stronger and more valuable.

Getting offers to sell also helped me realize the importance of solid accounting and the value of an outside audit. It's best to get independent audits to ensure that your numbers are accurate. Doing so will allow you to get a better market valuation and an objective view of your finances. It will also give you a better sense of what your business is really worth.

About the same time that more serious overtures were being made to buy my business, I had the opportunity to hear David Hammer give a presentation at our Entrepreneurs' Organization forum meeting about selling companies. I approached him after the speech, and we ended up having several discussions about the process of selling a company. He got me thinking more about looking at Planet Tan as an investor.

As I discussed in the previous tip, you've got to run your business as if you're going to run it for the long haul. At the same time, you've got to be able to switch gears so that you can also view your business strategically as an investor.

One of the first things viewing your business as an investor forces you to do is to ask yourself how the business can continue to run without you. The problem with most small to medium-size companies is that so much of the business is tied up in the drive and persona of the owner. At some point, you've got to be able to replace yourself as CEO.

In the last couple of years that I owned the business, I realized that I'd have to bring in the right people and build processes that would prepare the company to continue once I was gone. At that point, we made the decision to bring some key talent on board. We hired Dawn Byers as our business intelligence manager; we brought in Eva Thomas, a high-level CFO, to build a more robust accounting department; and Bernie Beck, an outstanding operations leader and all-around amazing guy who had been at Comp USA for over a decade, to help with our staff and systems.

Bernie made it possible for us to grow more quickly in the last year, because he put a training program in place that allowed us to groom store managers more quickly. Managers became responsible for training their own replacements so we'd always have someone on deck to take over a new location. Thanks to the team and the new leaders that came in to help take Planet Tan to the next level, we had amazing success during the last year of my ownership, when we added six new locations.

I also need to give special acknowledgment to one of the greatest cultural heroes in the company, Tom Peterson. Tom started as an assistant manager and, after a string of successes, became our marketing director after ten years with the company. Tom was not only a hero but also a huge cheerleader for the Planet Tan culture. If I wanted to show people what our ideal team member should look like, I would introduce them to Tom. During this final transitional period of my ownership, Tom was truly a key player.

And I can't forget Jason Spears, a district manager who has been with the company for ten years as well. Jason was a cultural go-to guy who could be counted on in any situation to come through on a project. Jason actually worked for me when I was just starting out in managing health clubs in Iowa and later made the move to Dallas to join Planet Tan.

I would like to give special thanks to our accounting partner, Montgomery Coscia Greilich LLP. Tom Montgomery was at many times our fractional CFO and helped us look at our business through a strategic financial lens. Last but not least, I would like to include Kent Billingsley of The Revenue Growth Company. Kent totally changed the way we thought about strategy, and as a result, everyone on the team was better aligned, which at the end of the day helped our revenue grow much faster.

Dawn Byers was instrumental in our growth as a company, putting new systems in place that would automate ordering and parts and materials. We borrowed the Six Sigma philosophy from General Electric and Jack Welch. For example, the Six Sigma standard in relation to tanning beds meant that we wanted to have 99 percent of our beds up and operational. That meant that out of 700 tanning beds, we never wanted to have more than seven off-line at any given time.

Dawn created a tracking device and worked with our maintenance department and our director of asset management to get an accurate read on how much of our tanning equipment was up and running. Once we had a clear picture, we realized that more than 25 percent of our beds were down at any given time. With the new system that Dawn put in place, we were able to go from 25 percent of the beds being off-line to almost 100 percent of the beds up and running on average. She had helped us get more strategic and proactive about parts and repairs, and we were able to use the technology and tracking to create a better level of service.

Two years out from the sale, we started thinking much more strategically, going out to find these high-level hires, and making big decisions that would grow the company. We were putting the right technology and software in place. Our culture started changing for the better, and we started to become more data driven. We started tracking and measuring more so we could find and fix weak areas. We had brought in bright, driven, and committed people with the right skill sets. By the time I had made the decision to sell the company, Planet Tan's future prospects were brighter than at any other time in the history of the company; we had the right people on board and the right systems in place. Rapid growth was happening.

Our future looked better than ever, and that's the position you want to be in when you are an entrepreneur considering selling your business. Because the company's prospects looked great, we knew we could sell from a position of strength.

Once I became more interested in the idea of selling, I brought in David Hammer, the business broker I had spoken with at the EO forum, so we could begin to explore our options more seriously.

Working with David, we could determine a fair market value for the business and decide what was best not just for me, but for the future of Planet Tan. After you put so much of yourself into a business for so many years, it's impossible to simply walk away without knowing the business can prosper well into the future without you. It felt like the right time for me to transition to the next chapter of my life, but before I made the transition, I wanted to ensure that my people would be taken care of.

I had devoted my entire working life to Planet Tan, and I was ready to explore other things life had to offer. After twenty-one consecutive years of almost nonstop work, I felt ready for whatever was next. The business had been my sole mission since college, often at the expense of everything else. As a lifelong learner, I knew there was still so much to be learned. Before selling the company, I had begun pursuing new and diverse interests — from glassblowing to running marathons to learning to fly. Selling the company from a position of strength and momentum would secure my financial future so that I could finally devote more time to my other new passions. I also wanted to travel and pursue some life goals outside of building a business. I knew that the time had come to exit the stage.

The timing of the decision to sell felt right. Planet Tan was at the top of its game, and I was feeling as though I had finally accomplished all I had set out to do. I loved the process of building a business from the ground up; the creation process was energizing and inspiring. I enjoyed the creative challenges and the complex mechanics of creating a business that worked. I knew that I had been engaged in something meaningful, and I had the emotional and personal satisfaction of having done something I was passionate about.

As I reflected on the possibility of selling the business, I came to realize that true success was not about money or how many stores we had; it was about being engaged in meaningful work. I had been fortunate that Planet Tan provided not only financial rewards but also emotional satisfaction. Still, as an entrepreneur at heart, I enjoyed the creation process more than the operational aspects. The business had scaled and matured, and I was beginning to consider other personal challenges. I felt great about where we had taken Planet Tan, but it was time for me to think about the next chapter of my life.

As the sale became a reality, I could not have written a better script for the way it all came together. Palm Beach Tan, my friendly competitor, agreed to buy the company. There was great synergy between the businesses, and we both felt we were getting excellent deals. Despite the bad economy at the time, Planet Tan was growing rapidly and operating like a well-oiled machine. The right people at Planet Tan had been groomed and were in a position to maintain our momentum. All the people who had been with me for years would benefit greatly from the sale, either with better jobs with the new company, or with greater opportunities elsewhere. It was really important to me to bring my team past the finish line with me, because that was always the way we operated—and the sale should be no different. Taking care of your team is more than the right thing to do; it also sends a message about your real values. You've got to look after the people you love.

I was so happy to see the team that I built do so well after the sale. Many of our key people were promoted to bigger roles, while other managers landed jobs with greater pay and responsibility at other companies. They had new opportunities and better situations almost across the board.

And for those who didn't have a place to go right away—I took them with me! I wasn't going to abandon them. In fact, I had the entire accounting department on my personal payroll until they found new opportunities! The sale was a win for everyone. I could walk away feeling proud of what we all had accomplished, and I could bow out gracefully knowing that the future of Planet Tan was bright.

One of my lifetime goals that I had committed to over twenty years earlier was to be able to retire at age forty. I wanted to secure my financial future early enough in life to pursue other goals. Well, I missed that goal—but only by thirteen days! My forty-first birthday was November 5, and the sale of Planet Tan was official on November 18. It was close enough that I was pleased with my accomplishments. Plus, I was ready to tackle new challenges, travel to all the places I had always wanted to explore, and pursue new adventures . . .

As I write this, I can tell you there has not been one day since the sale that I have not thought about the business that was such a big part of my life for thirteen and a half years. I've had emotional highs . . . and the feeling of losing my best friend.

The decision to sell is never an easy one, and it usually isn't black and white. Depending on the goals of the owner—whether building a company that can survive long after the owner's demise or the thrill of building something exciting that may one day lead to financial good fortune—the best way to structure a sale varies from situation to situation. The only thing I can say for sure, based on my personal experience, is this: When faced with the opportunity to change my financial life forever, it was important for me to secure the situation for my family and myself. I still have the drive to run another company, but taking away the financial pressure would free me up to compete from a position of strength in the next business opportunity I undertake.

In summary, it's scary to take on risk when all of your personal net worth is tied to the business. But that's what it's all about: The one that weighs in fully with the risk should be the one who benefits from the eventual triumph!

I hope that someday you will be faced with such a fantastic dilemma—that all of your hard work will provide you with the sort of exciting options I have been so lucky to experience. I believe in the entrepreneurial spirit of this country, and I know that the promise of better times ahead is for real!

Key Insights on Delivering on the Promise

- Consider the five key areas in which one company can compete. Does your business try to be the best in all of them? Which one should you focus on? How might tightening your business focus improve the company? Do customers get an "experience" from your company? What is the demographic of your clientele? How, specifically, do you accommodate them?

- Whether you are just starting to design the look of your company or are redesigning a new location, it's important to know what you do *not* want. Rule out certain components, and then look to designs you admire for inspiration. What are some examples of company designs you want to avoid? Which ones do you admire?

- Are you at the point in your company's life to "expand the brand"? Does your business have a mascot? What qualities would your team's cheerleader and symbol possess? How might having a mascot help to expand your brand? What would go into your company's brand bible? What are your promise, personality, and association? Make a list of "Your Company" vs. "Not Your Company" brands.

- Is your company involved in charity work? Develop a list of local organizations where your business could volunteer time and money. What kind of message does it send the community when your company participates in nonprofit work?

- Have you ever been approached to sell your company? Did that affect the way you ran the business? Why is it important to run your company as if you will own it forever? On the flip side, have you considered when you would be ready to sell? Have you ever thought about your company as an investor? Are you a risky brand or a stable one? Could the company run without you?

EPILOGUE

A Brand-New Chapter

Selling Planet Tan was a bit like watching your kid go off to college: This is what you've always wanted, and yet somehow you feel a little empty inside now that it's happening. After working my entire adult life on the one enormous and all-consuming endeavor of building a business, I was suddenly free of my responsibilities as a CEO. I was proud to leave a legacy at Planet Tan and to know that I had achieved my professional goals and assisted others on their own paths to success. Planet Tan is doing quite well today under the ownership of Palm Beach Tan. They have maintained the prestigious sponsorships of Dallas professional sports teams and continue to build their positive reputation in the community. Many of the models we implemented, such as Betty the mascot and the trademark hip and sassy marketing approach, continue to operate. But most importantly, the heart and soul of Planet Tan is still in place—its people. The key people who were with me to help start and grow the business continue to work in equal or greater roles at Planet Tan.

With the sale final and my former business thriving, I had the time, financial freedom, and flexibility to follow new dreams and literally explore the world. In many ways, I was starting a whole new life. I didn't retire in the traditional sense; instead, I set off to get reinspired. In addition to realizing a personal goal of traveling the world, I identified organizations of socially conscious entrepreneurs and found ways to get involved with them.

Although I had participated in charity work through Planet Tan, I now had a much larger portion of time and resources available to give back. I had a lot of different goals in life, and I didn't always know how I could achieve them all; often they seemed in competition with each other. How could I run and grow a successful business, have time to see exotic places, visit family and friends, and contribute to the greater good in the world—all at once? What I realized after I sold Planet Tan was that my goals were all possible, but only at different phases of my life. As they say, "All things in their season." The season of waking up early, staying up late, and having zero time for anything but business was finally over. It was time to reap the personal rewards of my long hours and to use my finances and knowledge to benefit others.

My first order of business was a twelve-month, twelve-country tour, with close friends joining me along the way. I explored everything from the heights of mountains to the depths of my own soul. As paradoxical as it sounds, I rest through activity, so my days were filled with physical exertion. I hiked through Patagonia in Argentina, ran in a marathon in Dallas, and cycled through the countryside in Italy. My business had frequently taken me away from people I loved and cared about, but now I had the chance to weave them back in.

One of the highlights of my trip was when my friend and former colleague Dave Taylor surprised me with a trip to London, Scotland, and Prague. Dave had worked with me at Planet Tan on two separate occasions as my CFO and as a trusted financial adviser over the entire thirteen and a half years we were in business.

When I met Dave at the train station in London, we gave each other a big hug. It was a real magical moment between good friends and business partners to celebrate our accomplishments by going on this amazing, once-in-a-lifetime trip. We took a train to Scotland, where we set off on a six-day hiking expedition through the magnificent Scottish Highlands. We hiked the Great Glen Way, the famous seventy-three-mile trail that follows the Caledonian Canal from Fort William to Inverness, and we hiked Ben Nevis, the highest peak in the British Isles. Dave went the extra mile and arranged a private tour of Stonehenge. We walked the grounds with only a handful of other people. It is truly beyond description to explain what it felt like to sit on the rocks and ponder the start of civilization. Sacred places such as this have a certain mystical quality. When you can sit back, be still, and absorb the gravity of the moment, you know that you are a part of something bigger than yourself. I had already climbed the metaphorical mountains in my professional life, and now I was able to unwind by conquering the physical heights with one of my dear business partners and friends.

I wanted to stay on my game mentally and physically through my travels and to grow as a person. Honestly, I hadn't quite figured out what to do next with my life. I knew the trip would keep me sharp and keep me learning. You have crazy ideas about the present and the future when you are traveling; I didn't say no to any of them. I wanted to keep them all in the running and mix it up like a big bowl of jambalaya in my mind.

For the first time in twenty years, I wasn't seeing everything through the lens of my business. My experiences were based on adventure, food, people, and travel, not profit margins or data matrices. During this time, I reflected on how best to contribute to the greater good of the world in a sustainable way. I didn't want to just write a check to a good cause; I wanted my life to be a good cause.

As I was beginning to hit my traveling stride and was at a place where anything seemed possible, my world came to a screeching halt when my mother's health took a turn for the worse. On July 1, I was finishing a cycling trip in the Piedmont in Italy and preparing to visit friends in Pamplona, Spain, to run with the bulls. Then I learned my mom's fight with cancer was quickly advancing. Suddenly, my travel plans changed. I was on a plane home to Dallas the next day.

For three weeks I was at my mom's side. We discussed everything from my mom's childhood to where we were in our lives on that very day. Most importantly, I was able to express my love, care, and respect for her one last time. When a person reaches the end stages of life, she senses the finality of it all. My mom was very much aware of what was happening, and she was at peace with it. It was such a blessing to be with her at the end, to cover seventy-five years' worth of life in twenty-two days and leave nothing unsaid between us. You really never know how much time on earth you have, and I feel extremely fortunate that my mom and I were able to savor those last few weeks for the precious gift that they were.

Everything I ever did in business, from my first entrepreneurial effort in the lawn-mowing/snow-shoveling industry to the final days at Planet Tan, was for my mom. I owe all my success to her example and work ethic. My first priority was always to be there for my family, and I am so blessed to have seen my mom in her final hours. After she passed on, I took the rest of the summer off to grieve and deal with my loss. Then I hit the road again—because I knew Mom would've wanted me to.

After Planet Tan was sold and especially after my mom's passing, I had a yearning to do something more with my life. This book, in fact, is a conduit to give something back. As you already know, I didn't grow up with a lot of advantages. I wasn't born with a powerful social circle or the proverbial silver spoon in my mouth. But through people like my mom, virtual mentors found in books and magazines, and a close circle of personal friends and mentors, I learned a great deal about how to do business and life well. My hope is that this book will do in the lives of aspiring entrepreneurs a fraction of what Jack Welch and Peter Drucker's books did for me.

For that reason, I'm donating 100 percent of the proceeds from this book to the National Foundation for Teaching Entrepreneurship (NFTE), an organization that helps young people from low-income communities build their business skills and unlock their entrepreneurial creativity. In 2009, I started volunteering with NFTE's Dallas branch. The students immediately impressed me, as did the innovative work the organization was doing. Although I had already decided to commit to a nonprofit organization in a big way, I hadn't known which one to choose. Based on my experiences with NFTE, I could quickly tell that their purpose was on target with my personal goals and values.

After testing the water, I decided to jump in headfirst and join the board of directors. Soon after that, I decided to make NFTE the beneficiary of this book. Being on the board for NFTE illustrates how I have truly come fill circle: I once would have been a member of the target group for this organization, and now I am helping to shape its future.

One of NFTE's main goals is to identify students at risk of dropping out of high school and give them a reason to stay. The NFTE curriculum and training is provided at no cost to teachers who will educate and inspire students to take hold of their own destinies and follow their passions in life. While NFTE identifies certain students who have a passion for entrepreneurship, the goal of the organization goes beyond business. The organization seeks to teach young people to take responsibility for their future and work hard to set and achieve their goals—whatever they may be. Our goal as a board is to help them find a pathway to prosperity.

The value of having trusted peers and friends is incalculable in business. For the past eight years, I've had the privilege of being a part of the Entrepreneurs' Organization (EO), and I consider it one of the most important decisions I've ever made. EO is a global network of more than 7,300 business owners in forty-two countries. Their vision is "to build the world's most influential community of entrepreneurs." The most rewarding part of membership for me has been my forum, a group of eight like-minded local business leaders that has met once a month for several years. In my life, the forum has functioned like a high-level board of directors. We are able to give candid feedback on a variety of issues, from handling a divorce to hiring a new company president. I recommend EO membership to anyone who owns or runs a business.

I also continue to work with the Nexus Recovery Center; I am involved with the S.M. Wright Foundation; and I have become a guest lecturer at the Cox School of Business at Southern Methodist University. Teaching is a new passion of mine, and I relish spending time with the next generation of business leaders and entrepreneurs. As I've said before, the value of a good mentor cannot be overstated. I was fortunate enough in my early years in business to have people older and wiser than me who offered advice, encouragement, and a listening ear. I'm thrilled to return the favor by paying it forward with students of all kinds.

Another organization that caught my attention and garnered my participation is the Idea Village in New Orleans. I have maintained a residence in New Orleans for eight years, and I have a deep love for the culture and people there. The Idea Village exists to foster entrepreneurship in New Orleans. It provides support, education, and grants to local businesses in their infancy with the hope of retaining entrepreneurial talent. More than 75 percent of the organization's total funding is from private sources. Any company with a mantra that tells people "Trust your crazy ideas," and then provides the economic channels to do it, gets my vote! I've been humbled by the great work they have done since starting up in 2000, and I am honored to note their support of this book and its goals.

In light of all the negative attention business has been getting since the recession, I think it is important to consider the impact of socially conscious entrepreneurs and organizations. Nonprofit companies like NFTE and the Idea Village represent the very best of American business minds and ideals. They work to inspire and empower people through business education, and their impact is immeasurable.

While I enjoyed all the stages of building and running Planet Tan, my real passion is getting a new business off the ground. Once I had reached my goals with Planet Tan, I knew it was time to exit. But that doesn't mean my business days are over. I've stayed active in the corporate world by forming my own investment company. This allows me to invest in businesses led by great entrepreneurs and own a stake in several local Dallas companies while still looking out for my next big business venture.

In fact, I can't think of anywhere I'd rather be for the foreseeable future than Dallas. Although I grew up in Illinois, I love doing business in Dallas because of the attitude here that anything is possible. There are so many people in the business and finance industry who encourage entrepreneurial involvement in the city. At an EO conference I attended in Dallas in May 2010, President George W. Bush said he moved to Dallas because, "there is no other place like it on earth." The energy and networking fiber of Dallas makes me want to live and work here for a long time to come.

After touring the world and writing a book, the time seems right to get back into a more strategic and active role in business. I am looking at several opportunities in the Dallas area that will allow me to work with businesses that help people feel and perform better. In this economic climate, thriving businesses are working to make people's lives better. Failing businesses are simply competing like everybody else in industries that don't directly affect the way people live. The ideas I've developed and honed during the past twenty years are transferrable to different kinds of businesses, and I look forward to taking on my next challenge. I consider myself extremely fortunate to have had the opportunity to explore new places, to meet fascinating new people, and to continue to learn new things. It's my thirst for knowledge and my natural curiosity that keep me excited about the future!

APPENDIX 1

Planet Tan's Plan for Success

It has often been said that a picture is worth a thousand words. I certainly found this to be true when I wanted to communicate key concepts to my team at Planet Tan. In this appendix you'll find some of the charts, graphics, and visuals that we used to create a culture of success at Planet Tan. You'll notice many of the concepts in the book recapped here in a more visual form. I highly recommend studying them and figuring out ways to apply them in your enterprise.

SUCCESSFUL FORMULA FOR HIRING A TOP PERFORMING TANNING CONSULTANT

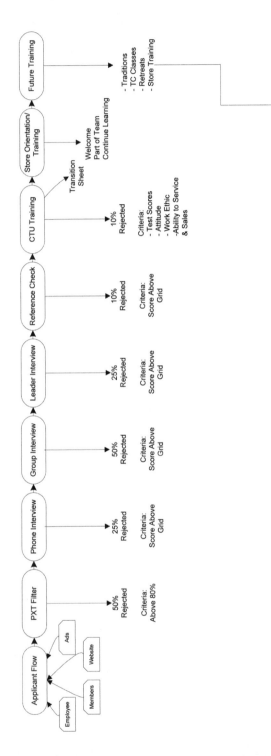

It all starts with people. As you can see, most of the prospective team members for Planet Tan were weeded out before they were hired. We wanted to make sure we were hiring the best, brightest, and most motivated. This was absolutely key to our amazing performance results.

MANAGEMENT PIPELINE

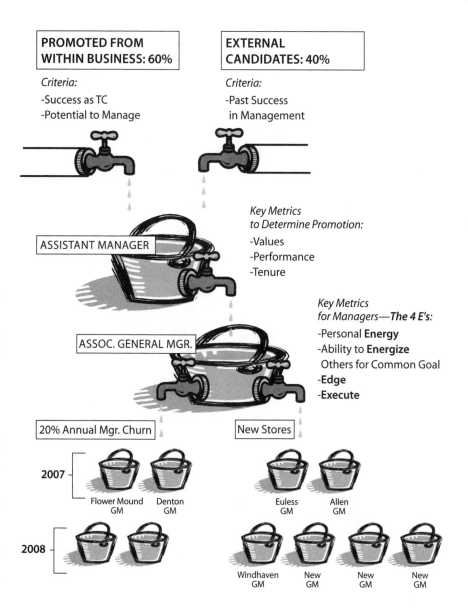

PROMOTED FROM WITHIN BUSINESS: 60%

Criteria:
-Success as TC
-Potential to Manage

EXTERNAL CANDIDATES: 40%

Criteria:
-Past Success
 in Management

ASSISTANT MANAGER

*Key Metrics
to Determine Promotion:*
-Values
-Performance
-Tenure

ASSOC. GENERAL MGR.

*Key Metrics
for Managers—The 4 E's:*
-Personal **Energy**
-Ability to **Energize**
 Others for Common Goal
-**Edge**
-**Execute**

20% Annual Mgr. Churn

New Stores

2007

Flower Mound
GM

Denton
GM

Euless
GM

Allen
GM

2008

Windhaven
GM

New
GM

New
GM

New
GM

As you can see, our aim was to find 60 percent of our company leadership from within our ranks, but also to be aware of stars-in-the-making who might come into the company from outside.

Decisions Diagram

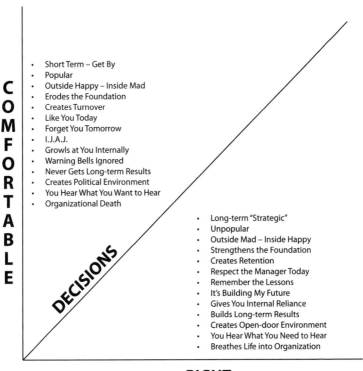

**C
O
M
F
O
R
T
A
B
L
E**

- Short Term – Get By
- Popular
- Outside Happy – Inside Mad
- Erodes the Foundation
- Creates Turnover
- Like You Today
- Forget You Tomorrow
- I.J.A.J.
- Growls at You Internally
- Warning Bells Ignored
- Never Gets Long-term Results
- Creates Political Environment
- You Hear What You Want to Hear
- Organizational Death

DECISIONS

- Long-term "Strategic"
- Unpopular
- Outside Mad – Inside Happy
- Strengthens the Foundation
- Creates Retention
- Respect the Manager Today
- Remember the Lessons
- It's Building My Future
- Gives You Internal Reliance
- Builds Long-term Results
- Creates Open-door Environment
- You Hear What You Need to Hear
- Breathes Life into Organization

RIGHT

One big reason the majority of people aren't as successful as they want to be — and it doesn't really matter what field of endeavor is under consideration — is because most people will not consistently choose being right over being comfortable.

10 -Year BHAG

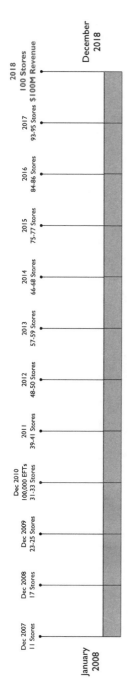

Dec 2007	Dec 2008	Dec 2009	Dec 2010	2011	2012	2013	2014	2015	2016	2017	2018
11 Stores	17 Stores	23-25 Stores	100,000 EFTs 31-33 Stores	39-41 Stores	48-50 Stores	57-59 Stores	66-68 Stores	75-77 Stores	84-86 Stores	93-95 Stores	100 Stores $100M Revenue

January
2008

December
2018

Setting goals is a fundamental attribute shared by all the truly successful people I know. Otherwise, desired results can degenerate into little more than wishful thinking. At Planet Tan, we set "Big, Hairy, Audacious Goals" (BHAGs), and then created an action plan to achieve them.

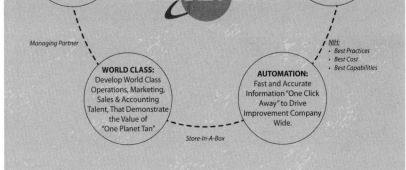

Our unique "Execute for Growth" focus was the yearly plan that provided the focus on specific performance objectives needed to help us meet our "BHAG."

APPENDIX 2

Recommended Reading

If you've read this far, you can't have missed the fact that I believe in continuous, lifelong learning. With that in mind, I offer the following list of outstanding books to help you stay informed, challenged, and focused.

Business Books

Innovation and Entrepreneurship, by Peter Drucker. Harper Paperbacks, 2006.

Managing for Results, by Peter Drucker. Collins, 1993.

Jack: Straight from the Gut, by Jack Welch. Business Plus, 2003.

Winning, by Jack Welch. HarperBusiness, 2005.

The Myth of Excellence: Why Great Companies Never Try to Be the Best at Everything, by Fred Crawford and Ryan Mathews. Three Rivers Press, 2003.

The Servant: A Simple Story about the True Essence of Leadership, by James Hunter. Prima, 1998.

Small Giants: Companies That Choose to Be Great Instead of Big, by Bo Burlingham. Portfolio Trade, 2007.

The Service Profit Chain: How Leading Companies Link Profit and Growth to Loyalty, Satisfaction, and Value, by James L. Heskett, W. Earl Sasser Jr., and Leonard A. Schlesinger. Free Press, 1997.

The Five Dysfunctions of a Team, by Patrick Lencioni. Jossey-Bass, 2002.

Why We Buy: The Science of Shopping, by Paco Underhill. Simon & Schuster, 2008.

The 80/20 Principle: The Secret to Success by Achieving More with Less, by Richard Koch. Broadway Business, 1999.

Business Culture Books

Business Stripped Bare: Adventures by a Global Entrepreneur, by Richard Branson. Virgin Books, 2010.

Pour Your Heart into It: How Starbucks Built a Company One Cup at a Time, by Howard Schultz. Hyperion, 1999.

Corporate Religion, by Jesper Kunde. Financial Times/Prentice Hall, 2002.

Branding and Marketing Books

Permission Marketing: Turning Strangers into Friends and Friends into Customers, by Seth Godin. Simon & Schuster, 1999.

Ogilvy on Advertising, by David Ogilvy. Vintage, 1985.

Lovemarks: The Future Beyond Brands, by Kevin Roberts. PowerHouse Books, 2005.

Emotional Branding: The New Paradigm for Connecting Brands to People, by Marc Gobé. Allworth Press, 2010 (updated ed.).

Inspirational Books

My Personal Best: Life Lessons from an All-American Journey, by John Wooden. McGraw-Hill, 2004.

Think and Grow Rich, by Napoleon Hill. Tarcher, 2005 (revised, expanded ed.).

See You at the Top, by Zig Ziglar. Pelican Publishing Company, 1982.

Benjamin Franklin: An American Life, by Walter Isaacson. Simon & Schuster, 2004.

Relaxing Favorites

The Sun Also Rises, by Ernest Hemingway (various editions available).

A Moveable Feast, by Ernest Hemingway (various editions available).

Walden, by Henry David Thoreau (various editions available).

Fahrenheit 451, by Ray Bradbury (various editions available).

Preparing for Extended Travel

Vagabonding: An Uncommon Guide to the Art of Long-Term World Travel, by Rolf Potts. Villard Books, 2002.

Jupiter's Travels: Four Years on One Motorbike, by Ted Simon. Jupitalia Productions, 2005.

Long Way Down: An Epic Journey by Motorcycle from Scotland to South Africa, by Ewan McGregor and Charley Boorman. Atria, 2009 (reprint ed.).

The 4-Hour Workweek: Escape 9-5, Live Anywhere, and Join the New Rich, by Timothy Ferriss. Crown, 2009 (expanded, updated ed.).

Honeymoon with My Brother, by Franz Wisner. St. Martin's Press, 2006.

Advance Praise for *Selling Sunshine*:

"If you've dreamed of being a successful entrepreneur, *Selling Sunshine* provides an excellent blueprint for turning up the heat and making it happen. Tony Hartl has crafted an important book that I highly recommend for any committed business impresario."

—**Dean Lindsay**, author of *The Progress Challenge*

"If Tony Hartl were a stock, I'd be a buyer. I'm sure the value would soar. Far more important, I know the profits would be used to encourage others and enhance the community."

—**Franz Wisner**, author of the *New York Times* bestselling *Honeymoon with My Brother*

"Wow! Tony Hartl is the real deal! His personal 'rags to riches' story is inspiring and proves the American Dream is alive and well. But more than that, his well-written book of life lessons provides a wealth of tips that we can all learn from."

—**Craig Hall**, author of *The Responsible Entrepreneur* and lifelong serial entrepreneur in real estate, oil and gas, venture capital, and wine